DIANETICS
THE EVOLUTION OF A SCIENCE

L. RON HUBBARD

Bridge

Publications, Inc.

A
HUBBARD®
PUBLICATION

BRIDGE PUBLICATIONS, INC.
4751 Fountain Avenue
Los Angeles, California 90029

ISBN 1-4031-0538-3

Printed in the United States of America

DIANETICS:

DIANETICS MEANS
"THROUGH THE MIND"
OR "THROUGH THE SOUL"
(FROM GREEK *DIA*, "THROUGH"
AND *NOUS*, "MIND" OR "SOUL").
IT IS A SYSTEM OF COORDINATED
AXIOMS WHICH RESOLVE PROBLEMS
CONCERNING HUMAN BEHAVIOR
AND PSYCHOSOMATIC ILLNESSES.
IT COMBINES A WORKABLE
TECHNIQUE AND A THOROUGHLY
VALIDATED METHOD FOR
INCREASING SANITY, BY ERASING
UNWANTED SENSATIONS AND
UNPLEASANT EMOTIONS.

IMPORTANT
NOTE

In READING THIS BOOK, BE VERY certain you never go past a word you do not fully understand.

The only reason a person gives up a study or becomes confused or unable to learn is because he or she has gone past a word that was not understood.

The confusion or inability to grasp or learn comes AFTER a word that the person did not have defined and understood.

Have you ever had the experience of coming to the end of a page and realizing you didn't know what you had read? Well, somewhere earlier on that page you went past a word that you had no definition for or an incorrect definition for.

Here's an example. "It was found that when the crepuscule arrived the children were quieter and when it was not present, they were much livelier." You see what happens. You think you don't understand the whole idea, but the inability to understand came entirely from the one word you could not define, *crepuscule,* which means twilight or darkness.

It may not only be the new and unusual words that you will have to look up. Some commonly used words can often be misdefined and so cause confusion.

This datum about not going past an undefined word is the most important fact in the whole subject of study. Every subject you have taken up and abandoned had its words, which you failed to get defined.

Therefore, in studying this book be very, very certain you never go past a word you do not fully understand. If the material becomes confusing or you can't seem to grasp it, there will be a word just earlier that you have not understood. Don't go any further, but go back to BEFORE you got into trouble, find the misunderstood word and get it defined.

FOOTNOTES AND
DEFINITIONS

To HELP YOU COMPREHEND THE
material in this book, words that might be easily misunderstood
are defined as footnotes the first time they appear in the text.
Each word so defined has a small number to its right, and the
definition appears at the bottom of the page beside the
corresponding number.

Words sometimes have several meanings, but only the
meaning of the word as it is used in the text is given in the
footnote. Other definitions for the word can be found in a
dictionary.

A glossary is also provided for you at the back of this book
which includes all the footnoted definitions as well as other
terms that appear in the text. Beside each glossary definition
you will find the chapter in which it appears and the footnote
number, where applicable, so you can refer back to it if you
wish.

CONTENTS

INTRODUCTION

Dianetics: The Evolution of a Science was L. Ron Hubbard's first broad publication to describe his breakthroughs which unlocked the subject of the human mind.

It contains a summation and overview of his decades of research into man and life and details the discoveries, development, application and results as they happened, all leading to what became man's first practical and effective technology of the mind.

Even prior to publication of this work, advance word of L. Ron Hubbard's breakthroughs was already mushrooming. An unpublished thesis describing his findings had been widely circulated in 1948, and by early 1950 the groundswell had reached national proportions. Typical of this growing excitement was renowned columnist Walter Winchell's announcement that, "There is something new coming up in April called Dianetics. A new science which works with the invariability of physical science in the field of the human mind. From all indications it will prove to be as revolutionary for humanity as the first caveman's discovery and utilization of fire."

The much anticipated *Dianetics: The Evolution of a Science* was first published as a book-length feature in a national American magazine. Within days, the issue sold out, triggering an avalanche of more than 2,000 reader letters in the first two weeks. This paved the way for L. Ron Hubbard's definitive handbook on the subject, *Dianetics: The Modern Science of Mental Health*. Published the following month, it became an immediate and unstoppable national bestseller.

As we move into the twenty-first century, Dianetics has become a worldwide phenomenon, applied by people from all walks of life in more than 50 languages and 150 nations.

On the following pages is the remarkable work that started it all —L. Ron Hubbard's own account of the evolution, development and application of Dianetics. This is how it all began, *how* it works and *why* it works.

—*The Editors*

YOUR MIND'S POTENTIAL

CHAPTER ONE

YOUR MIND'S
POTENTIAL

THE OPTIMUM COMPUTING
machine is a subject which many of us have studied. If you
were building one, how would you design it?

First, the machine should be able to compute with perfect
accuracy on any problem in the universe and produce answers
which were always and invariably right.

Second, the computer would have to be swift, working
much more quickly than the problem and process could be
vocally articulated.

Third, the computer would have to be able to handle
large numbers of variables and large numbers of problems
simultaneously.

Fourth, the computer would have to be able to evaluate its
own data, and there would have to remain available within it
not only a record of its former conclusions but the evaluations
leading to those conclusions.

Fifth, the computer would have to be served by a memory
bank[1] of nearly infinite capacity in which it could store
observational data, tentative conclusions which might serve
future computations and the data in the bank would have to be
available to the analytical portion of the computer in the
smallest fractions of a second.

Sixth, the computer would have to be able to rearrange
former conclusions or alter them in the light of new experience.

---

1. **bank:** a storage of information, as in a computer where the data was once stored on a group or series
of cards called a bank.

Seventh, the computer would not need an exterior program director but would be entirely self-determined about its programing guided only by the necessity-value of the solution which it itself would determine.

Eighth, the computer should be self-servicing and self-arming against present and future damage and would be able to estimate future damage.

Ninth, the computer should be served by perception by which it could determine necessity-value. The equipment should include means of contacting all desirable characteristics in the finite world. This would mean color-visio,[2] tone-audio, odor, tactile[3] and self-perceptions—for without the last it could not properly service itself.

Tenth, the memory bank should store perceptions as perceived, consecutive with time received with the smallest possible time divisions between perceptions. It would then store in color-visio (moving), tone-audio (flowing), odor, tactile and self-sensation—all of them cross-coordinated.

Eleventh, for the purposes of solutions, it would have to be able to create new situations and imagine new perceptions hitherto not perceived and should be able to conceive these to itself in terms of tone-audio, color-visio, odor, tactile and self-sensation and should be able to file anything so conceived as imagined, labeled *memories*.

Twelfth, its memory banks should not exhaust on inspection but should furnish to the central perceptor of the computer, without distortion, perfect copies of everything and anything in the banks in color-visio, tone-audio, odor, tactile and organic sensations.

Thirteenth, the entire machine should be portable.

There are other desirable characteristics but those listed above will do for the moment.

It might be somewhat astonishing, at first, to conceive of such a computer. But the fact is, the machine is in existence. There are billions of them in use today and many, many more billions have been made and used in the past.

---

2. **visio:** the sense of sight.
3. **tactile:** the sense of touch.

In fact, you've got one. For we are dealing with the human mind.

The above is a generalization of the optimum brain. The optimum brain, aside from the fact that it is not always capable of solving every problem in the universe, basically works exactly like that. It should have color-visio (in motion), tone-audio (flowing), odor, tactile and organic memory recall. And it should have color-visio (in motion), tone-audio (flowing), odor, tactile and organic imagination, also recallable after imagining like any other memory. And it should be able to differentiate between actuality and imagination with precision. And it should be able to recall any perception, even the trivial, asleep and awake from the beginning of life to death. That is the optimum brain, that, and much much more. It should think with such swiftness that vocal pondering would be utterly unable to keep pace with a thousandth part of one computation. And, modified by viewpoint and educational data, it should be *always* right, its answers *never* wrong.

That is the brain you have, potentially. That is the brain which can be restored to you unless you have had some section of it removed. If it does not do these things, it is slightly out of adjustment.

It took a long time to arrive at the data that this was an optimum brain. In the beginning it was not realized that some people had color-visio (moving) recall, for instance, and that some did not. I had no idea that many people imagined, and knew they were imagining, in tone-audio, et cetera, and would have received with surprise the data that somebody could smell and taste last Thanksgiving's turkey when he recalled it.

In 1938, when the researches which culminated in *Dianetics* (Greek *dia*—"through," and *nous*—"mind" or "soul") were started in earnest, no such high opinion of the human brain was held. In fact, the project was not begun to trace brain function and restore optimum operation, but to know the key to human behavior and the code law which would reduce[4] all knowledge.

---

4. **reduce:** to bring into a certain order; systematize.

CHAPTER TWO

WHAT LIFE IS DOING

CHAPTER TWO

WHAT LIFE IS DOING

MY RIGHT TO ENTER THIS FIELD was an inquiring brain which had been trained in mathematics and engineering and which had a memory bank full of questions and far-flung observations.

It was the basic contention that the human mind was a problem in engineering and that all knowledge would surrender to an engineering approach.

And another primary assumption was made:

All answers are basically simple.

As it stands today, the science of Dianetics and its results—which are as demonstrable as the proposition that water, at fifteen pounds per square inch and 212°F, boils—is an engineering science, built heuristically[1] on axioms.[2] It works. That is the only claim for Dianetics or chemistry. They may not be true. But they work and work invariably in the finite world.

When the problem had been shuffled around, in the beginning, and when questions had been formulated to be asked of the universe at large, there was no concept of the optimum brain. Attention was fixed upon the *normal* brain. The *normal* brain was considered to be the optimum brain. Attempts were made, when work finally got around to the problem of the brain itself, to obtain results comparable with the normal mind. Minds became aberrated.[3] When restored they would be normal.

---

1. **heuristically:** characterized by the use of experimentation, evaluation or trial-and-error methods.
2. **axiom:** a self-evident truth that requires no proof.
3. **aberrated:** affected by *aberration:* a departure from rational thought or behavior; not sane. From the Latin, *aberrare*, to wander from; *ab*, away, *errare*, to wander.

"...when questions had been formulated
to be asked of the universe at large,
there was no concept of the optimum brain."

In fact, in the beginning, it was not even certain that minds could be restored. All that was required was an answer to existence and the reasons minds aberrated.

In a lifetime of wandering around, many strange things had been observed: the medicine man of the Goldi people of Manchuria, the shamans[4] of North Borneo, Sioux medicine men, the cults of Los Angeles, and modern psychology. Amongst the people questioned about existence were a magician whose ancestors served in the court of Kublai Khan[5] and a Hindu who could hypnotize cats. Dabbles had been made in mysticism, data had been studied from mythology to spiritualism. Odds and ends like these, countless odds and ends.

If you were constructing this science, where would you have started? Here were all the various cults and creeds and practices of a whole world to draw upon. Here were facts to a number which makes 10^{21} binary digits[6] look small. If you were called upon to construct such a science and to come up with a workable answer, what would you have assumed, gone to observe or computed?

Everybody and everything seemed to have a scrap of the answer. The cults of all the ages, of all the world seem, each one, to contain a fragment of the truth. How do we gather and assemble the fragments? Or do we give up this nearly impossible task and begin postulating[7] our own answers?

Well, this is the story of how Dianetics was built. This, at least, was the approach made to the problem. Dianetics works, which is what an engineer asks—and it works all the time, which is what nature demands of the engineer.

First, attempts were made to discover what school or system was workable. Freud did occasionally. So did Chinese acupuncture. So did magic healing crystals in Australia and miracle shrines in

---

4. **shaman:** a priest or priestess who is said to act as an intermediary between natural and supernatural worlds and to use magic to cure ailments, foretell the future and to contact and control spiritual forces.
5. **Kublai Khan:** (1216–1294) the grandson of the founder of the Mongol dynasty, Genghis Khan, and who completed the conquest of China begun by his grandfather.
6. **10^{21} binary digits:** *binary* comes from a Latin word meaning *two at a time. Binary digits* refers to a system of numbering employed in computers which use only two numbers (digits), 0 and 1. *10^{21} binary digits* refers to an enormous quantity of 0s and 1s (1,000,000,000,000,000,000,000 of them) strung out one after another, forming a huge number.
7. **postulating:** assuming to be true, real or necessary, especially as a basis for reasoning.

South America. Faith healing, voodoo, narcosynthesis[8] ... And, understand this right here, no mystic mumbo jumbo need apply. An engineer has to have things he can measure. Later the word *demon* is used. That's because Socrates describes one so well. Dianetic use of it, like Clerk Maxwell's,[9] is descriptive slang. But no wild immeasurable guesses or opinions were wanted. When an engineer uses only those, bridges break, buildings fall, dynamos[10] stop and a civilization goes to wrack.

A primary need, in arriving at a dynamic[11] principle of existence, was to discover what one wanted to know about existence. One does not have to dabble long with the gods to know that they point unvaryingly, if divinely, up a very blind alley. And an engineering study of mysticism demonstrates that mysticism embraces largely what it cannot hope to state precisely.

The first proposition went off something on this order. Let us find out what we cannot consider or do not need to consider to get an answer we can use. Some tests seemed to demonstrate that the exact identity of the Prime Mover Unmoved[12] was not necessary to the computation. Man has been convinced for a long time that He started this affair, so no great gain could be made in getting disputative[13] about it. Let us then take a level immediately below the Prime Mover Unmoved.

Now let us see what else falls into the category of data unnecessary to the computation. Well, we've studied telepathy, demons, the Indian rope trick[14] and the human soul and so far we have yet to find any constants[15] in this class of data. So let us

---

8. **narcosynthesis:** drug hypnotism whereby a patient undergoes psychotherapy while drugged and in a "deep sleep."

9. **Clerk Maxwell:** James Clerk Maxwell (1831–1879), Scottish physicist who, in order to graphically explain certain physical universe phenomena, invented a hypothetical creature (or demon) that he said controlled the motion of individual molecules of gas and caused them to act in specific ways he had observed.

10. **dynamo:** a machine that generates electricity.

11. **dynamic:** active, energetic, effective, forceful, motivating, as opposed to static.

12. **Prime Mover Unmoved:** according to the philosophy of Aristotle (384–322 B.C.), that which is the first cause of all motion in the universe, which itself does not move. The Prime Mover was said to be eternal, immaterial and unchangeable, and Aristotle considered the Prime Mover as divine thought, mind or God.

13. **disputative:** inclined to argue; quarrelsome.

14. **Indian rope trick:** a magic trick, Oriental in origin, in which a magician suspends a rope in midair which a person then climbs up and seemingly disappears.

15. **constant:** something that does not or cannot change or vary.

draw a line below that as our highest level of necessary information and now call this our highest line.

What do we have left? We have the finite world, blue serge suits, Salinas Valley, the Cathedral at Reims as a building and several decayed empires and roast beef for dinner. We have left only what we can perceive with no higher level of abstraction.

Now, how do we perceive and on what and with what? Ensues here a lot of time spent—1937—in computing out the brain as an electronic calculator with the probable mathematics of its operation plus the impossibility of such a structure capable of doing such things. Let us then rule out the necessity of knowing structure and use this as an analogy only which can become a variable in the equation if necessary.

Now what do we have? Well, we've been a little hard on demons and the human soul. These are popular but they refuse to stand out and submit to a thorough inspection and caliper[16] mensuration[17] and if they won't so cooperate, then neither will we. And so two things come from this reduction of equation factors necessary to solution. First, existence is probably finite and second, finite factors alone answered the need of the problem.

Probably we could be very obtuse and mathematical here, but no matter. A good, workable, heuristic principle, a *workable* one, is worth an infinity of formulas based on Authority and opinions which do *not* work.

All we can do is try the principle. We need a dynamic principle of existence. We look in Spencer[18] and we find something which reads awfully good. It read good when he took it from Indian writings, the same place Lucretius[19] got it. But it only pretends to be dynamic because it doesn't compute. We need a *dynamic* principle, not a description.

16. **caliper:** a precise measuring instrument having two curved legs or jaws that can be adjusted to determine thickness, diameter and distance between surfaces.
17. **mensuration:** the action of measuring.
18. **Spencer:** Herbert Spencer (1820–1903), English philosopher known for his application of the scientific doctrines of evolution to philosophy and ethics.
19. **Lucretius:** (ca. 98–55 B.C.) Roman poet who was the author of the unfinished instructional poem in six books, *On the Nature of Things*, which set forth in outline a complete science of the universe.

But what does a principle mean in a sphere this large? And doesn't it need a better definition? Let us then call it a dynamic lowest common denominator of existence.

Will such a lowest common denominator lead us straight up above the highest level we have set and send us spinning off with a fist full of variables and no answer? It had better not. So let us pose some more questions and see if they clarify the principle.

What can we know? Can we know where life came from? Not just now. Can we know where life is going? Well, that would be interesting but few of us will live to see that. So what can we know? Who, when, why, where, what—WHAT! We can know WHAT life is doing.

Let us postulate now that life started somewhere and is going somewhere. To know *where* it came from might solve a lot of problems but that seems unnecessary to know at this time for this problem. And the somewhere might be known too some day but again we do not need to know that. So, now we have something for the equation which will stay in terms of constants. WHAT is life doing en route?

Life is energy of some sort. The purpose seems to involve energy. We are being heuristic. No arguments necessary because all we want is something with a high degree of workability—that's all any scientist needs. If this won't work, we'll dream up another one and postulate and postulate until something does work.

What is energy doing? It's surviving—changing form, but surviving.

What is life doing? It's surviving.

Now, maybe it is doing a whole lot more, but we'll just try this on for size. What is the lowest common denominator of all existence which we have so far found?

SURVIVE!

The only test of an organism is survival.

That can be computed.

We can even go so far as to make it colorful and say that there was a beginning of track and at this beginning of track

Somebody said SURVIVE! He didn't say why and He didn't say until. All He said was SURVIVE!

Well, that's simple and it computes. It makes sense on the slide rule and it makes sense with a lot of activity and it seems pretty good—let's see.

The brain was a computer-director evolved on the same principles and on the same plan as cells and by cells and is composed of cells. The brain resolved problems relating to survival, asked itself questions about survival, acted upon its own best-conceived but personally viewpointed plan for survival.

If one sagged down toward unsurvival, one was goaded up the scale toward survival by pain. One was lured ahead by pleasure into survival. There was a graduated scale with one end in death and the other in immortality.

The brain thought in terms of differences, similarities and identities and all its problems were resolved on these lines and all these problems and all these activities were strictly and solely survival motivated. The basic command data on which the body and brain operated was SURVIVE! That was all; nothing fell outside this.

It was postulated to see if it worked.

That was in 1938 after several years of study. The axioms began with SURVIVE! SURVIVE! was the lowest common denominator of all existence. They proceeded through axioms as to what man was doing and how he was doing it. Nice definitions for intelligence, drive, happiness, good, evil and so forth fell into line. Suicide, laughter, drunkenness and folly all fell inside this, too, as it computed out.

These computations stood the tests of several years. And then, as you may have heard, came a war. But even wars end. Research was resumed, but now with the added necessity of applying the knowledge gained to the problems of friends who had not survived the war too well.

❧

"DEMONS"
OF THE MIND

"DEMONS"
OF THE MIND

A RESEARCHER GETS OUT ON
a rim of the unknown just so far and the guidebooks run out. In
the libraries were thousands and thousands of mental cases,
neatly recorded. *And not one case contained in it the essential data
to its solution.* These cases might just as well have been written
in vanishing ink for all the good they were. Beyond proving
conclusively that people manifested strange mental aberrations,
they were worthless. How do you go about building a science of
thought without being permitted to observe and without
having any observed data?

Out of a multitude of personal observations in this and
distant lands, it was the first task to find a constant. I had
studied hypnotism in Asia. I knew hypnotism was, more or
less, a fundamental. Whenever shamans, medicine men,
exorcists[1] or even modern psychologists go to work, they
incline toward practices which are hypnotic.

But of what use is such a terrible, unpredictable variable as
hypnotism? On some people it works. On most it doesn't. On
those on whom it works it sometimes achieves good results,
sometimes bad. Wild stuff, hypnotism.

The physical scientist, however, is not unacquainted with
the use of a wild variable. Such erratic things usually hide real,

---

1. **exorcist:** one who drives out evil spirits (from a person or place) by religious or solemn ceremony.

important laws. Hypnotism was a sort of constant thread through all the cults—or hypnotic practices—but perhaps one might at least look at it.

So hypnotism was examined. A wild[2] radical.[3] The reason it was wild might be a good answer. The first investigation of it was quite brief. It did not need to be longer.

Examine a posthypnotic suggestion.[4] Patient in amnesia trance.[5] Tell him that when he awakens he will remove his left shoe and put it on the mantel. Then tell him that he will forget he has been told and wake him up. He awakens, blinks for a while and then puts his foot forward and removes his shoe. Ask him why. "My foot's too hot." He puts the shoe on the mantel. Why? "I hate to put on a damp shoe. Warmer up here and it will dry." Keep this in mind, this experiment. The full reason for its importance did not appear for nine years. But it was recognized that, with various suggestions, one could create the appearance of various neuroses, psychoses, compulsions and repressions listed by the psychiatrist. The examination promptly went no further. One had too few answers yet. But it was clear that *hypnotism and insanity were, somehow, identities.* A search was begun for the reason why.

For a long time and with many, many people, attempts were made to unlock the riddle. What caused hypnotism? What did it do? Why did it behave unpredictably?

Examination was made of hypnoanalysis.[6] It sounds good in the texts but it doesn't work. It doesn't work for several reasons, first among them being that you can't hypnotize everybody. Further, it works only occasionally, even when a person can be hypnotized. So hypnoanalysis was buried along

2. **wild:** unrestricted, uncontrolled, erratic, unsteady.
3. **radical:** a fundamental thing or character, basic principle.
4. **posthypnotic suggestion:** a suggestion made during hypnosis so as to be effective after awakening.
5. **amnesia trance:** a deep trance of a person in a sleep, making him susceptible to commands.
6. **hypnoanalysis:** a method of psychoanalysis in which a patient is hypnotized in an attempt to reach analytic data and early emotional reactions.

with the water cure[7] of Bedlam[8] and the prefrontal lobotomy[9] and the demon-extraction techniques of the shamans of British Guiana, and the search for the key which could restore a mind to normal was continued.

But hypnotism wouldn't stay quite dead. Narcosynthesis seemed a good lead, until some cases were discovered which had been "cured" by narcosynthesis. They were reworked with the technique just to discover what had occurred. Narcosynthesis sometimes seemed to fix a man up so his war neurosis could rise to even greater heights at some future date. No, that is not entirely fair. It produced slightly higher results than a magic healing crystal in the hands of an Australian medicine man. It seemed to do something beyond what it was supposed to do, and that something beyond was bad. Here was another wild variable, a piece of the puzzle of insanity's cause. We knew WHAT man was doing. He was surviving. Somehow, some way, he occasionally became irrational. Where did hypnotism fit into this? Why did drug hypnotism affect people so adversely at times?

These people one met and worked with did seem to be trapped somehow by something which modern methods almost never touched. And why did whole nations rise up to slaughter nations? And why did religious zealots carry a banner and crescent[10] across three quarters of Europe? People behave as if they'd been cursed by something. Were they basically evil? Was social training a thin veneer? Was the evil curse a natural inheritance from the tooth-and-claw animal kingdom? Was the brain *ever* capable of rationality? Hypnotism and narcosynthesis, unpredictable radicals, refused for a time to divulge answers.

7. **water cure:** a psychiatric treatment, purported to remove demons from a person whereby the patient was stretched out on the ground and had water poured into his mouth from some height.
8. **Bedlam:** an old insane asylum (in full, *St. Mary of Bethlehem*) in London, known for its inhumane treatment of its inmates.
9. **prefrontal lobotomy:** a psychiatric operation carried out by boring holes into the skull, entering the brain and severing the nerve pathways in the two frontal lobes, resulting in the patient becoming an emotional vegetable.
10. **banner and crescent:** a reference to the flag and crescent symbol of Muslim armies which, during the Middle Ages, conquered much of Europe.

Out of orbit again and without tools with which to work, it was necessary to hark back[11] to the techniques of the Kayan[12] shaman of Borneo, amongst others. Their theory is crude; they exorcise demons. All right. We postulated that man is evil, that the evil is native. Then we ought to be able to increase the civilized veneer by planting in him more civilization, using hypnotism. So the patient usually gets worse. That postulate[13] didn't work. Provisionally, let's try the postulate that man is good and follow its conclusions. And we suppose something such as the Borneo shaman's *Toh*[14] has entered into him which directs him to do evil things.

Man has believed longer that demons inhabit men than man has believed they did not. We assume demons. We look for some demons, one way or another. *And we found some!*

This was a discovery almost as mad as some of the patients on hand. But the thing to do was try to measure and classify demons.

Strange work for an engineer and mathematician! But it was found that the "demons" could be classified. There were several "demons" in each patient, but there were only a few classes of "demons." There were audio demons, subaudio demons, visio demons, interior demons, exterior demons, ordering demons, directing demons, critical demons, apathetic demons, angry demons, bored demons and "curtain" demons who merely occluded things. The last seemed the most common. Looking into a few minds established soon that it was difficult to find anyone who didn't have some of these demons.

It was necessary to set up an optimum brain. That brain would be postulated, subject to change. It would be the combined

---

11. **hark back:** to return or revert to some earlier point.
12. **Kayan:** people native to the island of Borneo. Settled mainly on the Kayan River, they worship many gods and practice shamanism.
13. **postulate:** a proposition that requires no proof, being self-evident, or that is for a specific purpose assumed true.
14. **Toh:** an agent of the spiritual world in primitive cultures. *Toh* are considered malevolent spirits and are blamed for disasters, such as crop failures, sickness and death.

"Man has believed longer that demons
inhabit men than man has believed they did not.
We assume demons. We look for some demons,
one way or another. And we found some!"

best qualities of all brains studied. It would be able to visualize in color and hear with all tones and sounds present, all memories necessary to thought. It would think without talking to itself, thinking in concepts and conclusions rather than words. It would be able to imagine visually in color anything it cared to imagine and hear anything it cared to imagine it would hear. It was discovered eventually that it could also imagine smells and tactiles but this did not enter into the original. Finally it would know when it was recalling and know when it was imagining.

Now, for purposes of analogy it was necessary to go back to the electronic computer idea conceived in 1938. Circuits were drawn up for the visio and audio recall, for color and tone recall, for imagination visio and audio creation and color and tone creation. Then were drawn the memory bank circuits. All this was fairly easy at this time since some extensive work had been done on this in the thirties.

With this diagram, further circuits were set up. The optimum brain was a plain circuit. To this were added the "demon" circuits. It was found that by very ordinary electronics one could install every kind of a "demon" that had been observed.

The "demons," since none of them consented to present themselves for a proper examination as demons, were, it was concluded, installed in the brain in the same way one would install a new circuit in the optimum brain. But as there was just so much brain, it was obvious that these electronic "demons" were using parts of the optimum brain and that they were no more competent than the optimum brain inherently was. This was more postulating. All one wanted was a good result. If this hadn't worked something else would have been tried.

Thus the solution was entered upon. While the human brain is a shade too wonderful an instrument to be classified with anything as clumsy as contemporary electronics, as marvelous as modern electronics are, the analogy stands. It stands as an analogy. The whole science would hang together brightly now without that analogy. But it serves in this place.

There are no demons. No ghosts and ghouls or *Tohs*. But there are aberrative circuits. So it was reasoned. It was a postulate. And then it became something more.

CHAPTER FOUR

THE BASIC
PERSONALITY

THE BASIC PERSONALITY

ONE DAY A PATIENT FELL ASLEEP. When awakened he was found to be "somebody else." As "somebody else" he was questioned very carefully. This patient, as "himself," had a sonic memory block, an audio memory block and was colorblind. He was very nervous ordinarily. Just now, awakened into being "somebody else," he was calm. He spoke in a lower voice tone. Here, obviously, one was confronting one of these electronic screw-ups the savants[1] call schizophrenics.[2] But not so. This was the basic personality of the patient himself, possessed of an optimum brain!

It was very rapidly established that he had color-visio recall on anything, tone-audio recall, tone-audio and color-visio imagination and entire coordinative control. He knew when he was imagining and when he was recalling and that, too, was something he had not been able to do before.

He wanted to know something. He wanted to know when the operator was going to help him get himself squared around. He had a lot of things to do. He wanted to help his wife out so she wouldn't have to support the family. How unlike the patient of an hour before!

He obligingly did some mental computations with accuracy and clarity and then he was permitted to lie down and sleep. He woke up with no recollection of what had happened. He had his

---

1. **savant:** a person of extensive learning.
2. **schizophrenic:** a person with two (or more) apparent personalities. *Schizophrenia* means *scissors* or *two*, plus *head*. Literally, *splitting of the mind*, hence, *split personality*.

"If man were basically good, then only a 'black enchantment' could make him evil. What was the source of this enchantment? Did we admit superstitions and demons as actualities and suppose the source was something weird and wonderful in the way of ectoplasm? Or did we part company with many current beliefs and become something a little more scientific?"

old symptoms. Nothing could shake those electronic blocks. He didn't even know if he had eaten lunch, the color of my scarf, and as for his wife, served her right for being a condemned woman.

This was a first introduction to basic personality. It was a long way from a last acquaintance. It was found that it was possible to contact optimum brain operation in a number of people.

And the basic personalities contacted were, invariably, strong, hardy and constructively good! They were the same personalities as the patients had in a normal state minus certain mental powers, plus electronic demons and plus general unhappiness. I found that a "hardened criminal" with an obvious "criminal mind" was, in basic personality, a sincere, intelligent being with ambition and cooperativeness.

This was incredible. If this was basic brain, then basic brain was good. Then man was basically good. Social nature was inherent! If this was basic brain . . .

It was. That is a "clear." But we pull ahead of the story.

People were uniformly miserable being aberrated. The most miserable patient on the rolls had an aberration that made her act "happy" and the most nervous *aberree*[3] one would ever care to encounter had a mastering aberration about being always "calm." She said she was happy and tried to make herself and everyone believe it. He said he was calm. He instantly flew into a nervous fit if you told him he wasn't calm.

Tentatively and cautiously a conclusion was drawn that the optimum brain is the unaberrated brain, that the optimum brain is also the basic personality, that the basic personality, unless

3. **aberree:** an aberrated person.

organically deranged, was good. If man were basically good, then only a "black enchantment"[4] could make him evil.

What was the source of this enchantment?

Did we admit superstitions and demons as actualities and suppose the source was something weird and wonderful in the way of ectoplasm?[5] Or did we part company with many current beliefs and become something a little more scientific?

The source, then, must be the exterior world. A basic personality, so anxious to be strong, probably would not aberrate itself without some very powerful, internal, personal devil at work. But with the devils and "things that go boomp in the night" heaved into the scrapheap, what did we have left? There was the exterior world and only the exterior world.

Good enough; we'll see if this works again. Somehow the exterior world gets interior. The individual becomes possessed of some unknowns which set up circuits against his consent, the individual is aberrated and is less able to survive.

---

4. **black enchantment:** an evil or wicked spell.
5. **ectoplasm:** in spiritualism, the vaporous, luminous substance, which is supposed to emanate from a medium during a trance.

CHAPTER FIVE

THE EXTERIOR WORLD AND INTERIOR ABERRATION

THE EXTERIOR WORLD AND INTERIOR ABERRATION

THE NEXT HUNT WAS FOR THE unknown factor. The track looked pretty fair, so far, but the idea was to formulate a science of thought. And a science, at least to an engineer, is something pretty precise. It has to be built on axioms to which there are precious few, if any, exceptions. It has to produce predictable results uniformly and *every time.*

Perhaps engineering sciences are this way because natural obstacles oppose the engineer, and matter has a rather unhandy way of refusing to be overlooked because someone has an opinion. If an engineer forms an opinion that trains can run in thin air and so omits the construction of a bridge across a stream, gravity is going to take over and spill one train into one stream.

Thus, if we are to have a science of thought, it is going to be necessary to have workable axioms which, applied with techniques, will produce uniform results in all cases and produce them invariably.

A great deal of compartmentation of the problems had already been done, as previously mentioned or in the course of work. This was necessary in order to examine the problem proper which was man in the universe.

First, we divided what we could probably think about and had to think about from what we probably didn't have to think about, for purposes of our solution. Next, we had to think about all men. Then a few men. Finally the individual man and at last a portion of the aberrative pattern of an individual man.

How did the exterior world become an interior aberration?

There were many false starts and blind passages just as there had been in determining what an optimum brain would be. There were still so many variables and possible erroneous combinations in the computation that it looked like something out of Kant.[1] But there is no argument with results. There is no substitute for a bridge heavy enough to hold a train.

I tried, on the off chance that they might be right, several schools of psychology—Jung, Adler. Even Freud.[2] But not very seriously because over half the patients on the rolls had been given very extensive courses in psychoanalysis by experts, with no great results. The work of Pavlov[3] was reviewed in case there was something there. But men aren't dogs. Looking back on these people's work now, a lot of things they did made sense. But reading their work and using it when one did *not* know, they didn't make sense, from which can be concluded that rearview mirrors six feet wide tell more to a man who is driving with a peephole in front than he knew when he was approaching an object.

Then came up another of a multitude of the doctrines, which had to be originated to resolve this work. *The selection of importances.* One looks at a sea of facts. Every drop in the sea is like every other drop. Some few of the drops are of vast importance. How to find one? How to tell when it is

---

1. **Kant:** Immanuel Kant (1724–1804), German philosopher who maintained that objects of experience (phenomena) may be known, but that things lying beyond the realm of possible experience are unknowable. Kant's works are often considered difficult to understand.

2. **Freud, Jung, Adler:** psychologists Sigmund Freud (1856–1939), Carl Gustav Jung (1875–1961) and Alfred Adler (1870–1937). Freud founded psychoanalysis and while Jung and Adler collaborated with him at first, both parted company and founded their independent schools of thought as they disagreed with Freud's emphasis on sex as a driving force. Jung theorized that all humans inherit a *collective unconscious*, which contains universal symbols and memories from their ancestral past, while Adler thought people were primarily motivated to overcome inherent feelings of inferiority.

3. **Pavlov:** Ivan Petrovich Pavlov (1849–1936), Russian physiologist, noted for his dog experiments. Pavlov presented food to a dog, while he sounded a bell. After repeating this procedure several times, the dog (in anticipation) would salivate at the sound of the bell, whether or not food was presented. Pavlov concluded that all acquired habits, even the higher mental activity of man, depended on conditioned reflexes.

"The selection of importances. *One looks at a sea of facts. Every drop in the sea is like every other drop. Some few of the drops are of vast importance. How to find one? How to tell when it is important?*"

important? A lot of prior art in the field of the mind—and as far as I was concerned, all of it—is like that. Ten thousand facts, all and each with one apparent unit importance value. Now, unerringly select the right one. Yes, once one has found, by some other means, the right one, it is very simple to look over the facts and pick out the proper one and say, "See? There it was all the time. Old Whoosis[4] knew what he was doing." But try it before you know! It's a cinch Old Whoosis did not know or he would have red-tabbed[5] the fact and thrown the others away. So, with this new doctrine of the selection of importances, all data not of personal testing or discovery was jettisoned. I had been led up so many blind alleys by unthorough observation and careless work on the part of forerunners in this business that it was time to decide that it was much, much easier to construct a whole premise than it was to go needle-in-the-haystacking.[6] It was a rather desperate turn of affairs when this came about. Nothing was working. I found I had imbibed,[7] unconsciously, a lot of prior errors which were impeding the project. There were literally hundreds of these "Why, everybody knows that———" which had no more foundation in experimentation or observation than a Roman omen.

So it was concluded that the exterior world got interior through some process entirely unknown and unsuspected. There was memory. How much did we know about memory? How many kinds of memory might there be? How many banks was the nervous system running on? The problem was not *where* they were. That was an off-track problem. The problem was *what* they were.

I drew up some fancy schematics, threw them away and drew some more. I drew up a genetic bank, a mimic bank, a

---

4. **Whoosis:** an indefinite or unspecified person or thing or one that is representative or typical.
5. **red-tab:** to use a red tab so as to identify or earmark for a specific purpose, the color red often being associated with urgent or emergency situations, usually as a warning.
6. **needle-in-the-haystacking:** from the expression "needle in the haystack" which refers to attempting to find a needle in a stack of hay—an extremely difficult or impossible task.
7. **imbibe:** to take or receive into the mind, as knowledge, ideas, or the like.

social bank, a scientific bank. But they were all wrong. They couldn't be located in a brain as such.

Then a terrible thought came. There was this doctrine of the selection of importances. But there was another, earlier doctrine—the introduction of an arbitrary.[8] Introduce an arbitrary and if it is only an arbitrary, the whole computation goes out. What was I doing that had introduced an arbitrary? Was there another "Why, everybody knows that——" still in this computation?

It's hard to make your wits kick out things which have been accepted, unquestioned, from earliest childhood—hard to suspect them. Another sea of facts, and these in the memory bank of the computer trying to find them.

There was an arbitrary. Who introduced it I don't know, but it was probably about the third shaman who practiced shortly after the third generation of talking men had begun to talk.

Mind *and* body.

There's the pleasant little hooker.[9] Take a good look at it. Mind *AND* body. This is one of those things like a ghost. Somebody said they saw one. They don't recall just who it was or where, but they're *sure . . .*

Who said they were separate? Where's the evidence? Everybody who has measured a mind without the body being present please raise both his hands. Oh, yes, sure. In books. I'm talking to you but I'm not there in the room with you right now. So mind is naturally separate from body. Only it isn't. A man's body can leave footprints. Those are products of the body. The products of the mind can also be viewed when the body is not there, but these are *products of* and the product of the object is not the object.

So let's consider them a unity. Then the body remembers. It may coordinate its activities in a mechanism called the brain, but the fact is that the brain is also part of the nervous system and the nervous system extends all through the body. If you

---

8. **arbitrary:** something derived from mere opinion; something unreasonable or unsupported.
9. **hooker:** a concealed problem, flaw, or drawback; a catch.

"A man's body can leave footprints. Those are products
of the body. The products of the mind can also be viewed
when the body is not there, but these are products of
and the product of the object is not the object."

don't believe it, pinch yourself. Then wait ten minutes and go back to the time you pinched yourself. Time travel back. Pretend you are all back there. You will feel the pinch; that's memory.

All right. If the body remembers and if the mind and body are not necessarily two items, then what memories would be the strongest? Why, memories that have pain in them, of course. And then what memories would be the strongest? Those which would have the most physical pain. But these are not recallable!

Maybe it's the wrong postulate, maybe people are in fifty pieces not just one, but let's try it on for size.

So I pinched a few patients and made them pretend they had moved back to the moment of the pinch. And it hurt them again. And one young man, who cared a great deal about science and not much about his physical being, volunteered for a nice, heavy knockout.

And I took him back to it and he recalled it.

Then came the idea that maybe people remembered their operations. And so a technique was invented and the next thing I knew I had a memory of a nitrous oxide[10] dental operation laid wide open and in recall, complete with pain.

10. **nitrous oxide:** a sweet-smelling, sweet-tasting gas used in dentistry and surgery to render the patient unconscious.

MISCONCEPTIONS ABOUT THE MIND

C H A P T E R   S I X

MISCONCEPTIONS ABOUT THE MIND

A GREAT DEAL OF EXPERIMENTATION and observation disclosed the fact that there were no moments of "unconsciousness." And that was another misconception which had held up man's progress.

"Unconsciousness." Someday the word will either be gone or have a new meaning because just now it doesn't really mean a thing.

The *unconscious mind* is the mind which is *always conscious*. So there is no "unconscious mind." And there is no "unconsciousness." This made modern psychology look like Tarawa[1] after the Marines had landed; for this is about as easy to prove as the statement that when an apple is held three feet in the air and let fall, it drops, conditions being normal.

It was necessary, then, to redraw all the circuit diagrams and to bring forth some terminology which would not be quite as erroneous as "unconsciousness" and the "unconscious mind."

For handy purposes, in view of the fact that I had gotten myself into difficulties before by using words with accepted meanings, I turned some adjectives into nouns, scrambled a few syllables and tried to get as far as possible from the focus of infection: Authority. By using old terms, one interposes, in communication, the necessity of explaining away an old

---

1. **Tarawa:** an island in the central Pacific Ocean captured from the Japanese by US Marines in 1943, after very heavy fighting.

meaning before he can explain the new one. A whole chain of thought can get thoroughly jammed up in trying to explain that while this word meant ——— it now means ———. Usually, in communications, one is not permitted to get beyond an effort to explain one does not mean ———.

Now there is no reason here to go into an evolution of terms in Dianetics. The cycle of the evolution is not yet complete. And so I will place here terms which were long afterwards conceived. They are not yet stet.[2] But their definitions are not quibbles: the order of definition is clear on the order of apples are apples.

The important thing is what we are defining. There were several heuristic principles on which the initial work was based which were "understood." One was that the human mind was capable of solving some of the riddles of existence. At this stage in the evolution of Dianetics, after "unconsciousness" had been smoked out of the "Why, everybody knows that ——— " class of information and labeled for what it was, an error, it was necessary to look over some of the "understood" postulates of 1938. And one of those "everybody knows" postulates has been that the human mind is not capable of understanding the workings of the human mind.

And "everybody knew that" the human mind was liable to err, that it was stupid, and was very easily aberrated by such small things as because Papa loved Mama, and Jimmy wanted to love Mama, too.

And "everybody knew that" the workings of the human mind were enormously complex; so involved that a complete direct solution of the problem was impossible. That, in effect, the human mind was a Rube Goldberg[3] device built up of an enormously unstable and delicately balanced pile of odd-shaped bits of emotion and experience, liable to collapse at any time.

2. **stet:** "let it stand," a printer's term used to indicate that matter previously marked for deletion is to remain.
3. **Rube Goldberg:** (1883–1970) American cartoonist known for his depiction of ridiculously intricate mechanical devices designed to accomplish absurdly simple tasks.

"And 'everybody knew that' the workings of
the human mind were enormously complex; so
involved that a complete direct solution of the
problem was impossible. That, in effect, the human
mind was a Rube Goldberg device built up of an
enormously unstable and delicately balanced pile
of odd-shaped bits of emotion and experience,
liable to collapse at any time."

From the engineering viewpoint, that seems a little strange. Two billion years of evolution, a billion successive test models, would tend to produce a fairly streamlined, functional mechanism. After that much experience, animal life would be expected to produce a truly functional mechanism—and Rube Goldberg's devices are amusing because they are so insanely nonfunctional. It somehow doesn't seem probable that two billion years of trial-and-error development could wind up with a clumsy, complex, poorly balanced mechanism for survival—and that jerry-built thing an absolute master of all other animal life!

Some of those "everybody knows that ———— " postulates needed checking—and checking out of the computation.

First, everybody knows that "to err is human." And second, everybody knows that we are pawns in the hairy grasp of some ogre who is, and always will be, unknown.

Only this didn't sound like engineering to me. I'd listened to the voodoo drums in Cap Haitien and the bullhorns in the lama temples of the Western Hills. The people who beat those drums and blew those horns were subject to disease, starvation and terror. Looked like we had a ratio at work here. The closer a civilization, or a man, moved toward admitting the ability of the human mind to compute—the closer the proposition was entered that natural obstacles and chaos were susceptible to orderly solution—the better he, or they, fared in the business of living. And here we were back with our original postulate again, SURVIVE! Now this computation would be warranted only if it worked.

But it was a not unwarrantable conclusion. I had had experience now with basic personality. Basic personality could compute like a well-greased UNIVAC.[4] It was constructive. It was rational. It was sane.

---

4. **UNIVAC:** (late 1940s to late 1950s) *Universal Automatic Computer:* the first electronic computer designed and sold to solve commercial problems.

And so we entered upon the next seven-league-boot stride[5] in this evolution. What was sanity? It was rationality. A man was sane in the ratio that he could compute accurately, limited only by information and viewpoint.

---

5. **seven-league-boot stride:** *(figurative)* an enormous leap in progress, significant forward motion, as if one had taken a step that was seven leagues. Such boots are found in a fairy tale allowing one to cover seven leagues (about 21 miles or 34 kilometers) in a single step.

THE ANALYTICAL MIND

CHAPTER SEVEN

THE ANALYTICAL MIND

WHAT WAS THE OPTIMUM BRAIN? It was an entirely rational brain. What did one have to have to be entirely rational? What would any electronic computer have to have? All data must be available for inspection. All data it contained must be derived from its own computation or it must be able to compute and check the data it is fed. Take any electronic calculator . . . no, on second thought, don't take them. They're not smart enough to be on the same plane with the mind because they are of a greatly sub order of magnitude. Very well, let's take the mind itself, the optimum mind. Compare it to itself. When did man become sentient?[1] It's not absolutely necessary to the problem or these results to know just when or where man began to THINK, but let's compare him to his fellow mammals. What does he have that the other mammals don't have? What can he do that they can't do? What does he have that they have?

All it takes is the right question. What does he have that they have? He does have something—and he has something more than they have. Is it the same order? More or less.

You never met a dog yet that could drive a car, or a rat that could do arithmetic. But you have men that couldn't drive a car, and men that couldn't do much better with arithmetic than a rat. How did such men vary from the average?

It seemed that the average man had a computer that was not only better, it was infinitely finer than any animal's brain. When something happens to that computer, man is no longer MAN but a dog or a rat, for purposes of comparison in mental power.

Man's computer must be pretty good. After all those millions of years of evolution, it should be—in fact it should, by this time,

---

1. **sentient:** conscious or capable of perceptions; consciously perceiving.

have evolved a perfect computer, one that didn't give wrong answers because it couldn't make a mistake. We've already developed electronic computing machines so designed, with such built-in self-checking circuits, that they *can't*, by their very nature, turn out a wrong answer. Those machines stop themselves and summon an operator if something goes wrong so that the computer starts producing a wrong answer. We know how to make a machine that would not only do that, but set up circuits to find the error, and correct the erring circuit. If men have figured out ways to do that with a machine already . . .

I had long since laid aside the idea that one could do this job by dissecting a neuron.[2] Dead, they don't talk. Now I had to lay aside the idea that the brain's structural mechanism could even be guessed at this stage. But working on the heuristic basis of what works, it is not necessary to know *how* it is done in terms of physical mechanism if we can show that it *is* done. It was convenient to use electronic circuits as analogs,[3] and the analogy of an electronic brain, because I knew the terms of these things. The brain may or may not run on electric currents; what things can be measured in and around it by voltmeters are interesting. But electricity itself is measured indirectly today. Temperature is measured by the coefficient of expansion[4] caused by temperature. Encephalographs[5] are useful working around a brain, but that doesn't mean that the brain is as clumsy and crude as a vacuum-tube rig.[6] This was a necessary step because if the problem were to be solved one had to suppose that the brain could be patched up, and with some method decidedly short of surgery.

2. **neuron:** a cell that transmits nerve impulses and is the basic functional unit of the nervous system; also called nerve cell.

3. **analog:** something having analogy to something else. An analogy is a similarity between like features of two things on which a comparison may be based.

4. **coefficient of expansion:** in physics, a change in volume, area or length of a material that accompanies a change in temperature. For example, in a traditional thermometer, the volume of liquid mercury expands or contracts as it is heated or cooled by temperature. The amount of mercury expansion or contraction determines how high or low the thermometer reads.

5. **encephalograph:** an instrument for measuring and recording the electric activity of the brain.

6. **vacuum-tube rig:** a reference to computers as they existed in the late 1940s. The vacuum tube was a device broadly used in electronics to control flows of electrical currents. It is called a vacuum tube because it is a sealed glass tube or bulb from which almost all the air had been removed in order to improve electrical flow.

So here was what I seemed to be working with: a computing machine that could work from data stored in memory banks, and was so designed that the computer circuits themselves were inherently incapable of miscomputation. The computer was equipped with sensing devices—the sensory organs—which enabled it to compare its conclusions with the external world, and thus to use the data of the external world as part of the checking feedback circuits. If the derived answers did not match the observed external world, since the computing circuits were inherently incapable of producing a wrong computation, the data used in the problem must itself be wrong. Thus, a perfect, errorless computer can use external world data to check the validity of and evaluate its own data input. *Only* if the computational mechanism is inherently error-proof would this be possible. But men have already figured out mechanically simple ways of making an error-proof computer—and if man can figure it out at this stage of the game, two billion years of evolution could *and would.**

The system of the error-proof computer is easily understood. Imagine a vacuum-tube computer circuit. If one tube fails to function properly, the computer will turn out wrong answers every time that tube is required in the computation circuit. But suppose we set up two identical computers; now if a vacuum tube fails, the two, running the same problem in parallel, will get different answers—which indicates at once that there is a defect somewhere. This system is used in present computers which, when the different answer situation arises, summon the operator. But if three computers simultaneously calculate in parallel on each problem, it is possible to determine not only that a defect exists in one computer chain, but also to determine which contains the defect, and what the correct answer is. Now the defective unit can be located and replaced by the machine itself. No machines man has made have that feature; it requires a triple unit, and units are too expensive. But man's brain uses some eighteen billion neurons; the brain can afford to run all problems in triplicate, and must to achieve an inherently error-free computer. Only by having an error-free computer can the immensely important function of data-evaluating be made possible. —LRH

How did the mind work? Well, to solve this problem we did not have to know. Dr. Shannon[7] commented that he had tried every way he could think of to compute the material in the memory bank of the brain, and he had been forced to conclude that the brain could not retain more than three months' worth of observations if it recorded everything. And Dianetic research reveals that everything is recorded and retained. Dr. McCulloch of the University of Illinois postulating the electronic brain in 1949 is said to have done some computation to the effect that if the human brain cost a million dollars to build, its vacuum tubes would have to cost about 0.1 cent each, that the amount of power it would consume would light New York City and that it would take Niagara Falls to cool it. To these competent gentlemen we deliver up the problems of *structure*. To date, Dianetics has not violated anything actually known about structure. Indeed, by studious application of Dianetic principles, maybe the problem of structure can be better approached. But at a swoop, we have all this off our minds. We are dealing with *function* and *ability* and the adjustment of that function to the end of obtaining maximum operation. And we are dealing with an inherently *perfect* calculator.

We are dealing with a calculator which runs entirely on the principle that it must be right and must find out why if it isn't right. Its code might be stated as, "And I pledge myself to be right first, last and always and to be nothing but right and never to be, under any circumstances, wrong."

Now this is what you would expect of an organ dedicated to computing a life-and-death matter like survival. If you or I were building a calculator, we'd build one that would always give correct answers. Now, if the calculator we built was also itself a personality, it would maintain that it was right as well.

Having observed this computer in its optimum state as the basic personality, the conclusion was very far from a mere postulate. And so we will call this computer the "analytical mind." We could subdivide things further and get complicated by saying that there is an "I"[8] as well as a computer, but this

---

7. **Shannon:** Dr. Claude E. Shannon (1916–), US mathematician whose work impacted upon the development of computer and communications technology.
8. **"I":** (in philosophy and other fields) the source of thinking; the person himself, as distinct from the body, who is aware of being self; the soul.

leads off in some direction or other which, as things work out, isn't of much use at this time. And so the "analytical mind" or the "analyzer" is a computer and the "I" for our purposes. All we want is a good *workable solution.*

The next thing we must consider is what apparently makes man a sentient being and that consideration leads us into the conclusion that possession of this analyzer raises man far above his fellow mammals. For as long as man is rational, he is superior. When that rationality reduces, so does his state of being. So it can be postulated that it is this analyzer which places the gap between a dog and a man.

Study of animals has long been popular with experimental psychologists, but they must not be misevaluated. Pavlov's work was interesting; it proved dogs will be dogs. Now by light of these new observations and deductions it proved more than Pavlov knew. It proved men *weren't* dogs. Must be an answer here somewhere. Let's see. I've trained a lot of dogs. I've also trained a lot of kids. Once I had a theory that if you trained a kid as patiently as you trained a dog, then you would have an obedient kid. Didn't work. Hm-m-m. That's right. It didn't work. The more calmly and patiently one tried to make that kid into a well-trained dog—"Come here" and he'd run away—hm-m-m. Must be some difference between kids and dogs. Well, what do dogs have that kids don't have? Mentally, probably nothing. But what do kids have that dogs don't have? A good analytical mind!

Let us then observe this human analytical mind more closely. It must have a characteristic dissimilar to animal minds—minds in lower orders of mammals. We postulate that this characteristic must have a high survival value, it is evidently so prominent and widespread and the analyzer—hm-m-m.

The analyzer must have some quality which makes it a slightly different thinking apparatus than those observed in rats and dogs. Not just sensitivity and complexity. Must have something newer and better. Another principle? Well, hardly a whole principle but . . .

The more rational the mind, the more sane the man. The less rational the mind, the closer man approaches in conduct his cousins of the mammalian family. What makes the mind irrational?

❧

CHAPTER EIGHT

TRACKING DOWN
IRRATIONALITY'S
SOURCE

C H A P T E R   E I G H T

TRACKING DOWN IRRATIONALITY'S SOURCE

I SET UP A SERIES OF EXPERIMENTS, using the basic personalities I could contact above or below the level of the aberrated personalities and in these confirmed the clarity and optimum performance of the basic computer. Some of these patients were quite aberrated until they were in a hypnotic amnesia trance at which time they could be freed of operator control. The aberrations were not present. Stutterers did not stutter. Harlots became moral. Arithmetic was easy. Color-visio, tone-audio recall. Color-visio, tone-audio imagination. Knowledge of what was imagination and what wasn't. The "demons" had got parked somewhere. The circuits and filters causing aberration had been bypassed, to be more precisely technical and scientific.

Now, let's postulate that the aberrative circuits have been somehow introduced from the external world—covered that ground pretty well, pretty solid ground.

And here's an answer. The introduced bypass circuits and filters became the aberrations in some way we did not yet understand. And what new complexion did this give the analyzer?

Further research tended to indicate that the answer might be contained in the term "determinism." A careful inspection of this computation confirmed observations. Nothing was violated. Did it work?

Let's postulate this perfect computer. It is *responsible*. It has to be responsible. It is *right*. It has to be right. What would make it wrong? Exterior determinism beyond its capacity to reject. *If it could not kick out a false datum it would have to compute with it.* Then, and only then, would the perfect computer get wrong answers. A perfect computer had to be *self*-determined within the limits of necessary efforts to solve a problem. No self-determinism, bad computation.

The machine had to be in a large measure *self-determined* or it would not work. That was the conclusion. Good or bad, did it lead to further results?

It did.

When exterior determinism was entered into a human being, so as to overbalance his self-determinism, the correctness of his solutions fell off rapidly.

Let's take any common adding machine. We put into it the order that all of its solutions must contain the figure 7. We hold down 7 and put on the computer the problem of 6 × 1. The answer is wrong. But we still hold down 7. To all intents and purposes here, that machine is crazy. Why? Because it won't compute accurately so long as 7 is held down. Now we release 7 and put a very large problem on the machine and get a correct answer. The machine is now sane—rational. It gives correct answers. On an electronic computer we short the 7 so it is always added in, no matter what keys are punched. Then we give the machine to a storekeeper. He tries to use it and throws it on the junk heap because it won't give correct answers and he doesn't know anything about troubleshooting electronics and cares less. All he wants is a correct total.

Admitting the analytical mind computation, and admitting it only so long as it works, where does it get a held-down 7—an enforced wrong datum?

Now, a computer is not necessarily its memory bank. Memory banks can be added and detached to a standard computer of the electronic type. Where do we look for the error? Is it in the memory bank?

The search for what was holding down 7 involved quite a little hard work and speculation and guesses. Some more work had to be done on the computer—the analytical mind. And then came what seemed to be a bright thought. Supposing we set up the whole computer as the demon. A demon that is always and invariably right. Let's install one in a brain so that the computer can project outside the body and give the body orders. Let's make the computer a circuit independent of the individual. Well, hypnotism has some uses. Good tool for research sometimes even if it is a prime villain in aberration.

Two things happened the moment this was done. The computer could direct the body as an "exterior entity" and draw on the memory banks at will for anything. *Seven was no longer held down.*

Naturally this was a freak test, one that could be set up only in an excellent hypnotic patient. And it could be installed only as a temporary thing.

This artificial demon knew *everything*. The patient could hear him when the patient was awake. The demon was gifted with perfect recall. He directed the patient admirably. He did computations by moving the patient's hand—automatic writing[1]—and he did things the patient evidently could not do. But why could it? We had artificially split the analyzer away from the aberrated patient, making a new bypass circuit which bypassed all the aberrated circuits. This would have been a wonderful solution if it had not been for the fact that the patient was soon a slave to the demon and that the demon, after a while, began to pick up aberrations out of the plentiful store the patient had. But it served to test the memory banks.

Something must be wrong about these banks. Everything else was in good order. The banks contained an infinity of data which appalled one in its very completeness. So there ensued a good, long search to find something awry in the banks. In amnesia sleep or under narcosynthesis, the banks could be very thoroughly ransacked. By automatic writing, speaking and clairvoyance[2] they could be further tapped.

---

1. **automatic writing:** writing performed by a person without his conscious intention or awareness often encouraged in order to make contact with the writer's unconscious, uncovering censored or hidden data.
2. **clairvoyance:** keenness of mental perception, clearness of insight; insight into things beyond the image of ordinary perception.

This was a mad sort of way to go about things. But once one started to investigate memory banks, so much data kept turning up that he had to continue.

There's no place here for a recital of everything that was found in the human memory bank, its completeness, exactness and minuteness or its fantastically complicated, but very smart cross-filing system. But a résumé is necessary of some high points.

In the first place, the banks contain a complete color-video record of a person's whole life, no matter the "demon" circuits. The last occlude or falsify. They do not alter the bank or the accuracy of the bank. A "poor" memory means a curtained memory, the memory being complete. *Every perception observed in a lifetime is to be found in the banks.* All the perceptions. In good order.

Memories are filed by time. They have an age and emotional label, a state-of-physical-being label and a precise and exhaustive record of everything perceived by organic sensation, smell, taste, tactile, audio and visio perceptics *plus* the train of thought of the analyzer of that moment.

There is no inaccuracy in the banks. Inaccuracy can, of course, be caused by surgery or injury involving actually removed portions. Electric shock and other psychiatric efforts are equivocal.[3] Prefrontal lobotomy is such certain and complete mind murder that one cannot be certain thereafter of anything in the patient except zombiism.

Anyway, the memory banks are so fantastically complete and in such good order behind the bypass circuits in any man not organically tampered with, that I very nearly wore out the rug trying to conceive it. Very well, there was something between the banks and the analyzer. Must be. The banks were complete. The circuits were intact. In any patient organically sound—and that includes all patients who have psychosomatic ills—the basic personality was apparently intact, the banks were intact. But the banks and the analyzer somehow did not track.

Well, let's take another look. This is an engineering problem. So far it has surrendered beautifully to engineering thought and

---

3. **equivocal:** of doubtful nature or character; questionable; dubious; suspicious.

computation. Apparently it should go right on surrendering. But let's look at Freud. There's his Censor.[4] Let's see if there's a censor between the banks and the analyzer.

That folded up[5] in about two seconds Mex.[6] The censor is a composite of bypass circuits and is about as natural and necessary to a human being as the fifth wheel on a monocycle.[7] There isn't any censor. Served me right for trying to lean on authority. In terms of authority, if you can spell it, it's right. In terms of engineering, if it can't be found and measured in some fashion, it's probably absent.

I rechecked the memory banks. How was I withdrawing data? I was using automatic writing for some, bypass circuit for others, direct regression[8] and revivification[9] on the old-line Hindu principle[10] for others. I set about trying to classify what kind of data I was getting with each method of recall. All of a sudden the problem fell apart. By automatic writing I was getting data not available to the analyzer. By bypass I was getting data not available otherwise. By regression and revivification, material was being procured only a little better than could be recalled by the tranced subject. The data I could check was found to be invariably accurate by any of these methods. What was the difference between automatic writing data and simple trance data?

I took a patient's automatic data and regressed him to its period. He could not recall it. The data concerned a broken leg and a hospital. I bucked him into the incident by main[11] force.[12]

The patient received a very sharp pain in the area of the old break.

---

4. **Censor:** (in early Freudian dream theory) the force that represses ideas, impulses, and feelings, and prevents them from entering consciousness in their original, undisguised forms.
5. **fold up:** to break down, collapse; to fail.
6. **Mex:** a half quantity of anything.
7. **monocycle:** a vehicle with one wheel.
8. **regression:** a technique by which part of the individual's self remained in the present and part went back to the past.
9. **revivification:** the reliving of an incident or some portion of it as if it were happening now.
10. **old-line Hindu principle:** reference to the regression and revivification techniques used in Asia for thousands of years. Unlike recent Western schools, which held regression to be possible only in tranced or hypnotized subjects, in Asia this ability was found to be inherent in the fully alert individual.
11. **main:** sheer, utmost.
12. **force:** persuasive power; power to convince.

This was a long way from hypnoanalysis. This was an effort to find an interposition[13] between memory banks and analyzer, not an effort to relieve "traumatic experiences."

And there was the answer. Why not? Very simple. It had been sitting right there staring at me since 1938. Oh, these six-foot-wide rearview mirrors! I had even made a law about it.

The function of the mind included the avoidance of pain. Pain was unsurvival. Avoid it.

And that's it—the way to hold down 7! You can hold it down with physical pain! The exterior world enters into the man and becomes memory bank. The analyzer uses memory bank. The analyzer uses the exterior world. The analyzer is caught between yesterday's exterior world now interior and today and tomorrow's exterior world, still exterior.

Can it just be that this analyzer gets its data on one perceptic circuit? Can it be that that perceptic circuit carries yesterday and today both? Well, however that may be, the analyzer certainly behaves to yesterday's interior world the same way it behaves to today's exterior world so far as the avoidance of pain goes. The law works both ways.

The analyzer avoids yesterday's pain as well as today's pain. Well, that's reasonable. If you avoid yesterday's pain in today's environment, you have a much better chance to survive. In fact... But see here, there's more to the problem than this. If the analyzer had a clear view of yesterday's pain it could better avoid it in today. That would be good operation.

That was the "flaw" in the machine. But it was a highly necessary "flaw." Just because an organism is built to survive, molded to survive and intended to survive does not mean that it will, as a matter of course, be perfect.

But the analyzer *was* perfect.

The banks were perfect.

The analyzer just plain wouldn't ever let the irrationalities of the exterior world inside as long as it could help it.

As long as it could help it!

---

13. **interposition:** something that assumes an intervening position; something that comes between two or more things.

"And that's it—the way to hold down 7!
You can hold it down with physical pain!
The exterior world enters into the man
and becomes memory bank."

CHAPTER NINE

THE VILLAIN
OF THE PIECE

CHAPTER NINE

THE VILLAIN
OF THE PIECE

I WAS PROBING NOW FOR THE villain of the piece. He was not found for a while. Many experiments were made. Efforts were made to make several patients well by simply breaking through the pain wall the analyzer was "seeking to avoid." A lot of painful incidents were broken, mental and physical anguish by the libraryful, and without much relief. The patients relapsed.

Then it was discovered that when a patient was bucked through a period when he was "unconscious," he showed some improvement. Then it was discovered that these "unconscious" periods were rather like periods of hypnosis driven home by pain. The patient responded as though the "unconscious period" had been posthypnotic suggestion!

From this series of experiments a prime datum was picked up. You relieve the pain and the "unconsciousness" and the suggestive power goes away. The subject did not have to have any of the mumbo jumbo of hypnosis in this "unconscious period." But every perceptic perceived tended to aberrate him.

I did not realize until then that I was playing tag with a hitherto unappreciated midevolution step in man. If he was once a pollywog, he had never lost any of the parts he had evoluted through. How does a fish think?

Well, let's see how a fish would respond to pain. He is swimming in brackish water of yellow color over a green bottom, tasting shrimp. A big fish hits him a whack, misses but does not kill him. Our fish lives to come back another day. This time he swims into an area of brackish water with a black bottom. He gets a little nervous. Then the water becomes a yellow color. The fish becomes very, very alert. He coasts along and gets over a green bottom. Then he tastes shrimp and instantly swims away at a terrific rate.

Now, what if man still had his lower-organism responses? Well, it seemed, on experiment, that he did. Drug him with ether[1] and hurt him. Then give him a whiff of ether and he gets nervous. Start to put him out and he begins to fight. Other experiments all gave the same conclusion.

Lower organisms can be precisely and predictably determined in their responses. Pavlov's dogs. Any dog you ever trained. The dog may have something of an analyzer too, but he is a push-button[2] animal. And so is man. Ah, yes, so is man. You know, just like rats.

Only man *isn't!* Man has a wide power of choice. Interfere with that wide power and there's trouble brewing. Aberrate him enough and he's unpredictably push-buttonable. Cut his brain out with a knife—and he can be trained to speak woof-woof for his food. But, by golly, you better cut pretty well to get a good, satisfactory, one hundred percent of the time woof-woof!

What happens when a man gets "knocked out"? He "isn't there." *But all the memory recordings during the period are.* What happens when you knock him half out? He does strange, automatic things. What happens when his analyzer is so aberrated that ... hey! Wait! How would you build a good, sensitive analyzer? Would you leave it connected to every

1. **ether:** a colorless liquid, having an aromatic odor and sweet, burning taste, used formerly as an inhalant anesthetic.
2. **push-button:** stimulus-response. From the action of pushing a button which mechanically and predictably opens or closes an electrical circuit; for example, a doorbell.

"How would you build a good, sensitive analyzer?
Would you leave it connected to every shock?
Huh-uh! You'd fuse it so it would live
to think another day."

shock? Huh-uh! You'd fuse[3] it so it would live to think another day. In an emergency, what kind of a response do you want? Automatic!

Stove hot, hand on stove, withdraw hand. Do you do a computation on that? No indeed. What withdrew the hand? The analyzer? No. What happened to the analyzer for an instant during the shock? The analyzer goes out of circuit and leaves a mechanical-determining director in full charge! A good, fast, identity-thinking[4] director.

The analyzer does not think in identities. It thinks in differences, similarities. When it loses its power to differentiate and thinks in identities ... No, it never does that. That's madness and the analyzer does *not* go mad. But something around here thinks in identities. Start working on a patient and find out that hash equals snow equals an ache in the knee ... That's identity thinking.

We don't know here what really happens to that analyzer. But we do know that we have found something which interposes between the banks and the computer. Something which thinks in identities, has a high priority over reason during moments of stress, can be found whenever a man is sent into some of yesterday's unconscious moments.

We know what it does now. It takes command when the analyzer is out of circuit. Whether or not it is the old style mind, which man did not shed while graduating to sentience by developing an analyzer, is beside the point. Whether or not it is a structural entity of a combination of "unconscious periods" is equally outside our concern here. We are working in function and we want answers that work every time.

---

3. **fuse:** *(figurative)* to install a device to protect against shock, overload, etc. From the field of electricity where in an electric circuit, a strip of easily melting metal is inserted, which melts (or "blows") and thus interrupts the electrical flow to prevent damage should the electrical current increase beyond a certain safe level.

4. **identity(ies):** exact sameness in qualities or characteristics; equivalent or equal. (See rest of chapter for description of *identity-thinking.*)

Call this the *reactive mind*. It is a mind which is constructed to work in moments of enormous physical pain. It is rugged. It works all the way down to the bottom and within a millimeter of death. Maybe it's almost impossible to build a sharply sentient mind which would operate under the terrible conditions of agony in which we find the reactive mind operating. Maybe the reactive mind . . . well, that's structure. Here it is as function.

The reactive mind thinks in identities. It is a stimulus-response mind. Its actions are exteriorly determined. It has no power of choice. It puts physical pain data forward during moments of physical pain in an effort to save the organism. So long as its mandates and commands are obeyed, it withholds the physical pain. As soon as the organism starts to go against its commands, it inflicts the pain.

The fish, had he failed to swim away when in a danger area where he had been attacked, would have been forced away by the crude mechanism of pain going into restimulation.[5] No-swim equals aching side. Swim equals all right.

The analyzer blows its fuses, as any good machine would, when its delicate mechanism is about to be destroyed by overload. That's survival. The reactive mind kicks in when the analyzer is out. That's survival.

But something must go wrong. This was a pretty good scheme of things. But it didn't always work.

Or it worked too well.

Thus were discovered the reactive memory bank and its total content, the *engrams* and their *locks*.[6] An engram is simply a period of physical pain when the analyzer is out of circuit and the organism experiences something it conceives to be or which

---

5. **restimulation:** a condition in which an approximation of the reactive mind's content or some part thereof is perceived in the environment of the organism.
6. **lock:** a situation of mental anguish. It depends for its force on the engram to which it is appended. The lock is more or less known to the analyzer. It's a moment of severe restimulation of an engram.

is contrary to its survival. An engram is received only in the absence of the analytical power.

When the analyzer is out of circuit, data of high priority value can pass, without evaluation by the analyzer, into the memory bank. There it becomes a part of the emergency bank. This is a red-tab bank, the reactive mind, composed of high priority, dangerous situations which the organism has experienced. The reactive mind has this bank as its sole source of information. The reactive mind thinks in identities with this red-tab bank. So long as the analyzer is *fully* in circuit, the red-tab bank is null and void. With the analyzer partially out of circuit— as in weariness, drunkenness, or illness—a part of this bank can cut in.

Let's begin to call "unconsciousness" a new word: *anaten*. Analytical attenuation.[7] There is greater or lesser anaten. A man goes under ether. He becomes anaten. He is hit in the jaw and is anaten.

Now, what does an engram contain? Clinical examination of this object of interest demonstrates that the engram consists of anaten, time, physical age, emotion, physical pain, and every percept in order of sequence. Words, sights, smells, everything that was there.

We had to organize a new subscience here to think about engrams properly. It's the science of perceptics. Know your general semantics?[8] Well, same organization, only we take in all the perceptics and we show where the meaning of each perceptic originates and why man can't nonidentify, with ease and aplomb, so long as he has engrams.

The automatic writing I was getting was straight out of engrams. That and bypass circuits would disclose data received

---

7. **attenuation:** the weakening or reduction in force, intensity, effect, quantity, or value.
8. **general semantics:** a highly organized philosophical approach to language, developed by Alfred Korzybski (1879–1950), which sought a scientific basis for a clear understanding of the difference between words and reality and the ways in which words themselves can influence and limit man's ability to think.

during anaten—engrams. And then I discovered that these engrams had a peculiar faculty. They could create their own circuits, parasitically using the host circuits.

Here's how an engram can be established: Mary, age two, knocked out by dog, dog bites. Content of engram: anaten; age two (physical structure); smell of environment and dog; sight of dog jaws gaping and white teeth; organic sensation of pain in back of head (hit pavement); pain in posterior; dog bite in cheek; tactile of dog fur; concrete (elbows on pavement), hot dog breath; emotion; physical pain plus endocrine response;[9] audio of dog growl and passing car.

What Mary does with the engram: She does not "remember" the incident but sometimes plays she is a dog jumping on people and biting them. Otherwise no reaction. Then, at age ten, similar circumstances, no great anaten—the engram is restimulated. After this she has headaches when dogs bark or when cars pass that sound like *that* car, but only responds to the engram when she is tired or otherwise harassed. The engram was first dormant—data waiting just in case. Next it was *keyed in*[10]—stuff we have to watch out for. Then it was thereafter restimulated whenever any combination of its perceptics appeared while Mary was in slight anaten (weary). When forty years of age she responded in exactly the same way, and still has not the slightest conscious understanding of the real reason!

Now let's consider what would have happened if Mary's mama had yelled something really choice, engramically speaking: "Be calm! Be calm! Oh, my darling, it's always this way. Get out! Get out!" Something Mama had tucked away as the proper thing to do and say, engramically, when dogs bite daughters.

9. **endocrine:** having to do with the secretion of hormones (chemical substances) from certain organs and tissues in the body. Some of these organs increase blood pressure and heart rate during times of stress.
10. **keyed in:** literally, a key is a small manual device for opening, closing or switching electronic contacts. *Key-in* is used here to describe a dormant engram that has activated and is now thrown into circuit.

We here have what amounts to a posthypnotic suggestion: *identity* (equals) *thought*. All the perceptics equal all the words equals a dog equals Mama equals get out, et cetera, et cetera, et cetera, and each equals all and any part of each. No wonder nobody could compute a madman! This is irrationality deluxe. Literally, this computation of *identity* thought makes no sense. But it's survival data and it better be obeyed or the cheek will hurt, the head will ache and the elbows will get a permanent "dermatitis."[11]

But remember that this engram also had, as a tab, anaten, the exact degree of anaten present during that moment. The analyzer is a fine device but it is also, evidently, a physical organ, probably the prefrontal lobes, and organic sensation includes several things. Restimulation brings about this state of affairs: "Analyzer shut off." "Reactive mind to cells. Red-tab dog in sight. Shut off analyzer. This is a priority situation. That is all."

The degree of anaten is very far from the original in the engram. But it is sufficient to produce a reduced state of analyzing, in effect a reduced sanity. The subject just has a feeling of dull, stupid mental confusion many times, a sort of dumb, unreasoned and unidentified emotion that seems to stop thought in numbness. You've had it! Thus we have a situation which begins to approach a push-button determinism. The engram which has become keyed in can, when the individual is slightly anaten—weary, ill, sleepy—be push-buttoned. Use the key word to the slightly anaten subject which is contained in one of his engrams and one of that engram's reactions may be observed. Push the button thoroughly enough and a full dramatization can be effected—he will *reenact* the original situation!

Thus the red-tab "memory" bank of the reactive mind. The discovery of this bank is one of the several original discoveries of Dianetics. Many parts of Dianetics can be found, if improperly evaluated, in old philosophic schools or in modern practice, but there remain a few entirely new facets which have no prior art.

11. **dermatitis:** inflammation of the skin resulting in redness, swelling, itching or other symptoms.

This red-tab bank is a very special affair and is quite different in composition, content and circuit from the analytical banks— conscious banks containing data which can be "remembered."

The reason this bank was never discovered before is not difficult to find. The red-tab bank content was implanted when the analyzer was out of circuit—unconscious. It is located, then, many strata below conscious awareness in the stupefactions[12] of a physical knockout. When one tried to get to it with hypnotism or narcosynthesis he was confronted with a patient who simply looked knocked-out, who was unresponsive to everything. As narcosynthesis and hypnotism both savor of sleep, the deeper sleep of the composite whole of all the past knockouts of a lifetime render the patient entirely insensible even when one was squarely on top of the reactive bank. So this bank remained hidden and unknown. And that is a sad thing because unless one knows about this bank the entire problem of man's imperfection, his insanity, his wars, his unhappiness, can go begging or get into the files of a shaman or a neurosurgeon. Much more widely, the hidden character of this bank can be said to be responsible for irrational conduct on the part of all mankind. And how many lives has that cost in the last four thousand years?

It is a very peculiar sort of a bank. It is the *only* bank in the human mind from which any content can be exhausted. All its content is pain and unconsciousness. And only physical pain can be deleted from the mind. Now, wouldn't you say that this was a peculiar sort of a bank? Here it is, with its bunkers full of high priority but false survival data. Here it is full of experiences which, because of the way they are filed, can drive a man to suicide or other madness. Here it is with its memories all ready to click into the motor controls of the body, ready, without so much as a by-your-leave[13] from the sentient analyzer, to make a man run insanely until he drops from heart failure. Here it is able to change the perfect structure of the body into a nightmare thing

---

12. **stupefaction:** a dazed or dull condition, where perception and understanding are blunted or deadened.
13. **by-your-leave:** an apology for not having sought permission.

with a fetuslike face and wasted or undeveloped limbs. Here it is ready to manufacture anything you can name by way of physical ills or at least to predispose them, possibly even cancer. Here it is filling hospitals, mental institutions and jails. And yet it is the one portion of human memory that can be modified and changed!

What price[14] some of the old philosophies when the only reducible "memory" is one of pain?

Try any technique you can name, on a pleasant or even a merely passing memory, in one of the conscious banks. It will stay right where it is, indelible, particularly the pleasurable ones. But a "memory" in the red-tab bank, when properly approached by Dianetic technique, will vanish out of that bank entirely. It refiles as a memory in the conscious level banks, and as such, by the way, is fantastically difficult to locate—on the order of what you ate for dinner on June 2nd when you were two years of age—and when found bears the tag "found to be nonsurvival data, do not permit it or similar data into any fundamental computations." And one of these unconscious "memories" when treated, produces about the same emotional response afterwards as a mildly amusing joke.

The red-tab bank could cause circuits to be set up which looked and sounded like demons. It could occlude the conscious bank in part or so thoroughly that it appeared that there was no past. It could command and order a person about like a moron might control a robot. And yet it is perishable. And it can be deintensified and refiled, with consequent great increase in the survival chances of a man. All its content is contrasurvival. When it is gone, survival is demonstrably enhanced—and that means what it says and the fact can be proven in a clinical laboratory with an experiment on the order of "Is this water?"

Pleasure memories can be attacked with various techniques. But they are set. They won't budge. Refile the reactive memories

---

14. **what price:** an expression or concept meaning "so much for"; what is the value of ———?

and the whole conscious lifetime of the individual springs into view, brilliant and clear, unmodified by the bypass circuits which are madness. Reduce the reactive bank and the optimum mind for the individual comes into view. The reactive bank was neither the drive nor the personality of the individual—these are indelible and inherent.

And another thing happens. The bypass circuits and the reactive bank apparently stand only between the conscious banks and the analyzer. They do not stand between, for instance, the ear and the sonic file in the conscious bank, the eye and the visio file, et cetera. This is a very important discovery in its own right, for it means that an aberration, for instance, about the inability to hear did not prevent all proper sounds from being filed, about the inability to see color did not prevent all color from being filed. Clear away the reactive circuit which apparently prevented the observations and the analyzer finds itself possessed of whole banks of material it never knew it had, all in proper sound and color et al.

For instance, a man who supposes that the whole world is ugly and sordid is guided through therapy. The aberration which made the world seem ugly and sordid folds up when the engram or engrams to that effect deintensify and refile. The bypass circuit these engrams caused to be set up did *not* prevent a full, true recording to be made via all sensory channels. Therefore, when the analyzer is permitted to enter the files, the individual discovers that he has innumerable pleasurable experiences which, when they occurred, appeared to him to be ugly and sordid, but which are now bright.

This postulates another circumstance, interesting but not vital to Dianetics. The standard memory banks of the mind are evidently not filled with memories which are entities capable of willy-nilly[15] determinism on the individual. They are not automatically restimulated by the perception of something which suggests them in the environment. They are not hooked

---

15. **willy-nilly:** whether one wishes to or not; willingly or unwillingly.

into circuit on a permanent basis at all. They are filled with conclusions and the analyzer may pick up the old conclusions or create new ones which change the old. In other words, *the standard bank is at the command of the analyzer and the individual; the individual is not at the command of the standard banks.*

In short, there is no such thing as conditioning. Conditioning is all right for rats and dogs and cats. They run on the reactive type bank. Therefore, what we refer to, ordinarily, as conditioning, is actually an engram command laid down in a specific moment. This is easily susceptible of clinical proof. The conditioning of a lifetime on the subject, say, of eating with a knife, breaks down the instant that the engram command demanding it is deintensified.

This is not theory, but actuality: Conditioning in the absence of engrams on the subject does not and cannot exist. Conditioning can be removed and will stay removed. There are, then, two things at work: The reactive mind commands certain actions and these can be altered by the deintensification of engrams. The analyzer can hook up and arrange certain automatic responses for various mechanical situations and actions. Call the reactive mind demand a habit, call the analytical requirement a training pattern. There are habits: These can be removed. There are training patterns: These can be altered only with the consent of the analyzer, which is to say, the individual. Practically all the survival patterns which really lead to survival are laid down on the analytical level. The reactions in which people indulge which are contrasurvival are laid down on the reactive level.

Conditioning, therefore, is another term which can be laid aside. The analyzer, working without impedance[16] by engrams, can lay down or take up training patterns at will. The reactive mind can lay down commands which make habits only when the exterior world implants such commands in the absence of full analytical power. Dianetics can break up habits, simply by

---

16. **impedance:** the preventing of progress; hindrance or something that delays or prevents progress.

relieving the engrams which command them. Dianetics could only change a training pattern if the individual consented to it.

These discoveries were an additional proof that man was a self-determined individual. Further investigation led to another finding: that although the reactive bank was exterior determinism, this determinism was a variable on the individual. In other words, the determinism laid in by pain had a variable effect. The same engram introduced into three different people might bring about three different reactions. Man is so thoroughly a self-determined organism that he has a variable reaction to all attempted determinisms. Research brought about the fact that he could exercise a power of choice over the reactive bank, even if in a limited manner. He had five ways to handle an engram: He could attack it and its counterpart in the exterior world, he could flee from it and its counterpart, he could avoid it and its counterpart, he could neglect it and its counterpart, or he could succumb to it. He was self-determined to some degree within this group of reactions. And these are the reactions to any dangerous, contrasurvival problem.

These are, by the way, known as the "black panther mechanisms" in Dianetic parlance. Imagine that a black panther is sitting on the stairs. There are five ways of handling the situation for a man sitting in the living room and who has a desire to go upstairs. He could attack the panther, he could flee from it, he could avoid it by going outside and coming up via the porch lattice—or entice the panther away as another method of avoidance, he could simply refuse to admit it was a black panther and attempt to go up anyway, or he could simply lie still in fear-paralysis and hope that the black panther would either eat him quietly, without too much pain, or merely walk off in antipathy to corpses. (Fear-paralysis, denial of dangerousness.)

Now, an analyzer does not handle conscious-level—standard bank—memories in this fashion. The analyzer evaluates the present and future in terms of *experience* and *education of the past* plus *imagination*. The standard bank is used for computation, not for emotional reaction, guilt, self-revilement, et cetera. The only

"He had five ways to handle an engram:
He could attack it and its counterpart in the
exterior world, he could flee from it and its
counterpart, he could avoid it and its counterpart,
he could neglect it and its counterpart, or he
could succumb to it....These are, by the way,
known as the 'black panther mechanisms'
in Dianetic parlance."

valid data is that data in the standard bank and in its search for success, happiness, pleasure or whatever desirable end, or merely in the art of contemplation, the analyzer must have reliable information and observation. It uses memory, conclusions drawn from experience and conclusions drawn from its conclusions and computes in various ways to obtain correct answers. It avoids a false datum as a curse once it knows it is false. And it is constantly reevaluating the memory files to reform conclusions. The more experience it has, the better its answers. Bad experience is fine data for computation because it brings in the necessity level.[17] But the analyzer *cannot* compute reactive data, the "unconscious memories" it cannot reach and does not even know about.

So these reactive "memories" aren't memories at all as we understand *memory*. They are something else. They were never meant to be recalled on the analytical level or to be analyzed in any way. The analyzer, trying to get around that red-tab bank, sets up some circuits which would tax a Goldberg to duplicate. The analyzer is trying to reach its proper conscious-level banks. If it can't, it can't compute right answers. If the analyzer keeps getting strange and seemingly sourceless material which nevertheless has pain to enforce its acceptance, that analyzer can get very wrong answers. And the structural body can go wrong. And motives go wrong. And somebody invents phrases like "It's human to err."

No, reactive "memories" aren't memories. So we call them by a good medical term, *engrams*—a lasting trace—and modify the definition by qualifying "lasting." They were certainly lasting enough pre-Dianetics.

The engram is received, we can postulate, on a cellular level. The engram is cellular memory by the cells and stored in the cells. We won't go further with this because at present we want to stay out of the problems of structure. But we can prove to

---

17. **necessity level:** the degree to which an individual feels the need or necessity to take a certain course of action.

anyone's satisfaction that the reactive mind bank is apparently inside the cells themselves, and is not part of the human mind banks which are composited of, we suppose, nerve cells. Engrams are in any kind of cell in the whole aggregation. They do not in the least depend upon nervous structure to exist. They use and prey upon nervous structure as we know it. So we are not talking about memory when we talk about engrams. We are talking about cellular recordings on the order of phonograph records, smell records, organic sensation records, all very precise. And when we say *reactive mind* we are talking about no special part of the body, but a composite, cellular-level moronic method of remembering and computing. Someday somebody may cut off a chunk of brain and cry, "Eureka, this is the reactive mind!" Possibly. But staying with our functional computation, we can make good time and get workable results. And so we need to know no seat[18] for the reactive mind. And we need to know nothing about the exact structure of its banks. All we want to know is what they do.

The reactive engram comes in with pain when the analytical mind is more or less out of circuit. The engram is *not* recorded in the conscious-level banks. It comes in on a cellular level, just as though the cells which compose the body, suddenly recognizing that the organism is in apparent danger of perishing, grab data in an effort to save themselves on the order of a disintegrated, every-man-for-himself effort. But the data they get is not disordered. It is most terribly precise, most alarmingly literal. It is exact. *Bean* means "bean" in all the ways the sound of "bean" can mean "bean."

Once received, this engram can then lie dormant, inactive. It takes a remotely similar, conscious-level experience to stir that engram up. This key-in moment evidently refiles the engram within the red-tab banks and gives it articulation. The words of the engram get meaning. The perceptions get hooked into the sensory organs. The engram is now in place. After this it can be

18. **seat:** a place in which something occurs or is established; physical location.

very easily restimulated. The cells are now capable of back-seat driving.[19]

By engram we mean, solely, the actual impression—like the indentations on a record[20]—of the "unconscious" experience upon the body.

Well, these are the discoveries. Once they had been made, it was necessary to find out how they could be applied.

19. **back-seat driving:** interfering in affairs from a subordinate position, giving unsolicited advice. From the practice of an automobile passenger offering a driver unsolicited advice, warnings, criticism, etc., especially from the back seat.
20. **record:** a reference to a phonograph record which consists of a disk with grooves in it.

CHAPTER TEN

DEVELOPMENT OF TECHNIQUE

CHAPTER TEN

DEVELOPMENT OF
TECHNIQUE

MAN, WE HAVE POSTULATED—
and it is certainly working—is obeying the basic command,
SURVIVE! This is a dynamic command. It demands action. In
looking over the matter of obedience to this command,
numerous computations were necessary. Survive. Well, the first
answer and the too obvious one is that man is surviving as a
unit organism. A very thorough computation on this—about
two hundred thousand words—revealed the fact that while
everything in the universe could be explained—by a few shifty
turns of logic—in terms of personal survival, the thing was
unwieldy and unworkable. We want things to be workable.
This is engineering, not idle study. We have a definite goal. So,
let us see if man is all out for man.

The whole reason for the organism's survival *can* be
computed down into this single effort, the survival of
contemporary mankind. All the reason a unit organism
survives is to let all mankind survive. But that does not work
well.

Now, let us take a group, under which we put symbiotes.[1]
Let us postulate that the unit organism survives wholly for the
group. Again, a computation can be made that explains
everything down to group. Group is the only reason, says this
computation. It's unwieldy, but there's nothing wrong with it.

---

1. **symbiotes:** organisms, persons, groups, etc., living in an interdependent or mutually beneficial
relationship. The atom depends on the universe, the universe on the atom.

All right, let's try bringing it all down to sex. And still it can be computed perfectly, if it is a trifle unwieldy. The reason man as a unit survives is to enjoy sex and create posterity. But it requires an enormous number of heavy, cumbersome manipulations of logic that no one would like.

Investigating in the mind—going to the object one is studying and really examining it instead of windily arguing about it and quoting authority—it was discovered that an apparent balance existed only when and if *all four drives* were relatively in force. Each one computed well enough, but taken as the fourfold goal they balance. The computing becomes very simple. Behavior begins to look good. Using all four, we can predict.

Now comes the proof. Can we use it? Does it work? It does. Engrams lie across these drives. They have their own energy, these engrams, a reverse polarity[2] surcharge[3] which inhibits the drive on which they lie. This is very schematic but it computes and we can use it in therapy. An unconscious period containing physical pain, and conceived or actual antagonism to survival, thwarts or blocks or impedes the flow of drive force. Begin to stack up these impedances on a drive and it begins to damp markedly.

Now comes arithmetic. There's a good reason to use the figure four. There are four drives. There are four levels of physical tone. If a man's composite drive force is considered as four and his restimulated—acute or chronic, either way— reactive mind force is high enough to reduce that composite drive force below two, *the individual is insane.* In view of the fact that an engram can be currently restimulated to reduce that force below two, a condition of temporary insanity results.

An engram can consist of Father beating Mother during a child's anaten. When this engram is highly restimulated, the

---

2. **polarity:** that quality or condition in a physical body or system that manifests opposite or contrasting properties, as in a magnet where one end is positive and the other negative. Reverse polarity refers to a state whereby two objects, conditions, etc., have opposing forces.
3. **surcharge:** an additional or excessive load or burden.

"There are four drives. There are four levels of physical tone. If a man's composite drive force is considered as four and his restimulated—acute or chronic, either way—reactive mind force is high enough to reduce that composite drive force below two, the individual is insane."

child, now an adult, may possibly dramatize it either as the father or the mother and will carry out the full drama, *word for word, blow for blow.*

In view of the fact that when Father beat Mother, Father was probably dramatizing one of his own engrams, another factor can be found here which is highly interesting. It is contagion. *Engrams are contagious.* Papa has an engram. He beats Mother into anaten. She now has an engram, word for word, from him. The child was anaten, maybe booted aside and knocked out. The child is part of Mother's perceptics for that engram. Mother dramatizes the engram on the child. The child has the engram. He dramatizes it on another child. When adulthood is attained, the engram is dramatized over and over. Contagion.

Why do societies degenerate? A race comes to a new place. New life, few restimulators—a restimulator being the environment's equivalent to the engram's perceptic content—and high necessity level which means high drive. The race thrives on the new frontier. And then begins this contagion, already present, brought in part from the old environment. And the descending spiral can be observed.

Having an engram makes one slightly anaten. Being slightly anaten one more easily receives new engrams. Engrams carry physical pain—*psychosomatics*[4]—which reduces the general tone and brings on further anaten. And in a rapidly descending spiral, the individual decays.

These were the computations achieved by research and investigation. Now it came to making them work. If they didn't work, we'd have to change things and get new principles. It happens that the above works.

But to start them working was a difficult thing. There was no way of knowing how many engrams a patient might have.

---

4. **psychosomatics:** body sensations, pains or discomfort stemming from the mind. Comes from *psycho* (mind) and *somatic* (body).

One could be cheerfully optimistic by this time. After all, there was a pretty good computation, some knowledge of the nature of the black enchantment, and it might be possible to bring about a "clear"—optimum working condition of the analyzer—in almost any patient. But the road was full of stones.

Several techniques were developed, all of which brought alleviation approximating a couple thousand hours of psychoanalysis. But that wasn't good enough. They could bring about better results than hypnoanalysis and bring them about much more easily. But that wasn't getting the train over the stream.

I found out about locks. A *lock* is a situation of mental anguish. It depends for its force on the engram to which it is appended. The lock is more or less known to the analyzer. It's a moment of severe restimulation of an engram. Psychoanalysis might be called a study of the locks. I discovered that any patient I had, had thousands upon thousands of locks, enough to keep me busy forever. Removal of locks alleviates. It even knocks down chronic psychosomatic ills—at times. It produces more result than anything else so far known elsewhere, but it doesn't *cure*. Removal of locks does not give the individual all his mental powers back, his audio-tone, visio-color, smell, taste, organic memory and imagination. And it doesn't particularly increase his IQ.[5] I knew that I was far from the optimum analyzer.

It was necessary to go back and back in the lives of patients looking for real engrams, total anaten. Many were found. Some were found that would release when the patient was removed in time back to them and was made to go over and over them, perceptic by perceptic. But there were also engrams that would not release, and they should have, if the original computation was correct. The optimum computer must analyze the data on which it operates, and, once false data have been called to its attention for questioning, the self-checking feature of the computer should automatically reject that falsity.

5. **IQ:** Intelligence Quotient, a number arrived at by means of intelligence tests and intended to indicate a person's intelligence.

The fact that an engram wouldn't release worried me; either the basic idea that the brain was a perfect computer was wrong, or—hm-m-m. Before too long it was found that one had to have the first engramic instant of each perceptic before the later engram would go. That looked like order. Get the earliest pain associated with, for instance, a squeaking streetcar wheel and later streetcar wheels, even in bad engrams, gave no trouble. The perfect computer wouldn't overcome the short circuit at level 256 if the same circuit was shorted at level 21, but clear the short circuit—the false data—where it first appeared, and then the computer could readily find and correct the later errors.

Then began the most persistent search possible to find the earliest engram in any patient. This was mad work. Utterly weird.

One day I found myself with a complete birth engram on my hands. At first I did not know what it was. Then there was the doctor's patter. There was the headache, the eyedrops . . . Hello! People can remember birth when they're properly bucked into it! Aha! Birth's the earliest engram. Everybody has a birth. We'll all be clears!

Ah, if it had been true! Everybody has a birth. And believe me, birth is quite an experience, very engramic, very aberrative. Causes asthma and eyestrain and somatics[6] galore. Birth is no picnic and the child is sometimes furious, sometimes apathetic but definitely recording, definitely a human being with a good idea of what's happening when he isn't anaten. And when the engram rises, he knows analytically all about it. (And he can dramatize it if he's a doctor, or she can dramatize it if she's a mother. Wow, lots of dope[7] here. Hot dope.) But birth isn't all the answer. Because people didn't become clears and stop stuttering and stop having ulcers and stop being aberrated and stop having demon circuits when birth was lifted. And sometimes birth didn't lift.

6. **somatics:** physical pain, discomfort, unwanted emotions or feelings coming from an engram.
7. **dope:** (slang) information, data, or news. Hot dope would be very exciting or interesting information.

"*Everybody has a birth. And believe me, birth is quite an experience, very engramic, very aberrative.*"

The last was enough for me. There was an axiom: Find the earliest engram. Know where it wound up? *Twenty-four hours after conception!* Not all cases, fortunately. Some cases waited four days after conception before they got their first engram. The embryo anatens easily; evidently *there's cellular anaten!*

No statement as drastic as this—as far beyond previous experience as this—can be accepted readily. I have no explanation of the structure involved; for the engineering answer of function, however, structural explanation is not immediately necessary. I was after one and only one thing; a technical process whereby aberrations could be eliminated, and the full potentiality of the computational ability of the mind restored. If that process involved accepting provisionally that human cells achieve awareness on the order of cellular engrams as little as a day or two after conception, then for the purposes at hand that proposition can, and must be, accepted. If it had been necessary to go back through two thousand years of genetic memory, I would still be going back to find that first engram—but fortunately there's no genetic memory, as such. But there definitely is something which the individual's mind regards as prenatal engrams. Their objective reality can be debated by anyone who chooses to do so; their subjective reality is beyond debate—so much so that the process works when, only when, and *invariably when* we accept the reality of those prenatal memories. We are seeking a process that cures aberrations, not an explanation of the universe, the function of life or anything else. Therefore we accept as a working—because it works—postulate that *prenatal engrams are recorded as early as twenty-four hours after conception.* The objective reality has been checked so far as time and limited means permitted. And the objective reality of prenatal engrams is evidently quite valid. Any psychologist can check this if he knows Dianetic technique and can find some twins separated at birth. But even if he found discrepancies, the bald fact remains that individuals *cannot* be rehabilitated unless the prenatal engrams are accepted.

What happens to a child in a womb? The commonest events are accidents, illnesses—and *attempted abortions!*

Call the last an AA. Where do people get ulcers? In the womb usually, AA. Full registry of all perceptics down to the last syllable, material which can be fully dramatized. The largest part of the proof is that lifting the engram of such an event can *resolve the ulcer!*

How does the fetus heal up with all this damage? Ask a doctor about twenty years hence—I've got my hands full. That's structure, and right now all I want is a clear.

What's that chronic cough? That's Mama's cough which compressed the baby into anaten when he was five days after conception. She said it "hurt" and "happened all the time." So it did. What's arthritis? Fetal damage or embryo damage.

It so happens, it is now known, that a clear can control all his body fluids. In an aberree, the reactive mind does a job of that. The reactive mind says things have to be such and so and that's survival. So a man grows a withered arm. That's survival. Or he has an inability to see, hysterical or actual blindness. That's survival. Sure it is. Good solid sense. Had an engram about it, didn't he?

What's TB? Predisposition of the respiratory system to infection. What's this, what's that? You've got the proposition now. It works. The psychosomatic ills, the arthritis, the impotence, this and that, they can go away when the engrams are cleared from the bottom.

That was the essence of the derivation of the technical process. With the research stage completed, the actual application was the remaining stage, and the gathering of data on the final, all-important question. The process worked—definitely and unequivocally worked. But the full definition of a science requires that it permit accurate description of how to produce a desired result *invariably.* Would the technique work on all types of minds, on every case?

CHAPTER ELEVEN

APPLICATION

CHAPTER ELEVEN

APPLICATION

BY EARLY 1950, OVER TWO hundred patients had been addressed; of those two hundred people, two hundred recoveries had been obtained. Dianetics is a science because by following readily prescribed techniques, which can be specifically stated, based on definitely stated basic postulates, a specifically described result can be obtained in every case. There may, conceivably, be exceptions to the technique now worked out, but I tried honestly to find exceptions and did not; that's why I tried so many cases, of so many different types. And some of them were really gruesome cases.

Who is an aberree? Anybody who has one or more engrams. And since birth itself is an engramic experience—every human being born has at least one engram!

The whole world, according to the hypnotist, needs nothing but to be hypnotized. Just put another engram, an artificial one, into a man, even if it's a manic engram—makes the subject "big" or "strong" or "powerful" plus all other perceptics contained—and he's all right. That's the basic trouble— reduction of self-determinism. So we don't use hypnotism. Besides, it's not workable on any high percentage. If you've followed this far without realizing that we are trying to wake up an analyzer, you made the same mistake I did for many months. I tried to work this stuff with hypnosis. Well, it works, after a sloppy fashion. But, how you put a man to sleep who is already three-quarters asleep—normal, near as I can discover—is a problem I wish could be solved. But fortunately it doesn't need solution.

The analyzer went to sleep with each engram. Each engram had lock engrams—like it, also engrams, but subsequent to it—and each chain of engrams—same species, people have about fifteen or twenty chains on the average of ten or fifteen engrams to the chain—has about a thousand locks. There are luckless people who have hundreds of engrams. They may be sane. There are people who have twenty engrams and are insane. There are people who are sane for years and suddenly get into just the right environment and get restimulated and go mad. And anybody who has had an engram fully restimulated has been mad—*vox populi*[1]—for at least once, even if only for ten minutes.

When we start to treat a patient, we are treating a partially asleep analyzer—and the problem is to wake him up in the first engram and then erase—that's right, *erase,* they vanish out of the reactive bank on recounting over and over with each perceptic—all subsequent engrams. The locks blow out without being touched, the Doctrine of the True Datum working full blast and the analyzer refusing to tolerate what it suddenly notices to be nonsense. And as he recovers mental function enough to reach back a little way into his past, we begin to alleviate. Then we finally find out the reactive mind plot (why he had to keep on being aberrated) and we blow out the demons—upsetting the circuits—and all of a sudden we are at *basic-basic,* first engram. Then we come forward, recounting each engram over and over until it blows away and refiles as *experience* as opposed to *command.*

---

1. *vox populi:* popular sentiment or the expressed general opinion. *Vox populi* is a Latin phrase which literally means "voice of the people."

A clear has regression recall. Basic personality, in an aberree, isn't strong enough to go back so we use what we call the *Dianetic reverie*.[2]

We found why narcosynthesis is so sloppy. It puts the partially restimulated engram into full restimulation, keys all of it in. The drug turns off the somatic—physical pain—so that it doesn't wholly go away. And narco[3] has no chance of going back far enough to get basic-basic and the one it reaches will pretend to erase and then will surge back in from sixty hours to sixty days.

Does any special thing hold up a case? Yes, the sympathy computation. Patient had a tough engramic background, then broke his leg and got sympathy. Thereafter he tends to go around with a simulated broken leg—arthritis, et cetera, et cetera. These are hard to crack sometimes, but they should be cracked first. They make a patient "want to be sick." Sickness has a high survival value says the reactive mind. So it tailors up a body to be sick, good and sick. Allies are usually grandmothers who protested against the child being aborted—effort already made, child listening in, not knowing the words just then, but he'll know them later when he knows his first words—nurses who were very kind; doctors who bawled Mama out, et cetera, et cetera. Patient usually has an enormous despair charge[4] around the loss of an ally. That'll hold up a case.

We've completely bypassed how this ties in with modern psychology. After all, modern psychology has labels for many observed conditions. How about schizophrenia, for instance?

---

2. **reverie:** a light state of "concentration" not to be confused with hypnosis; in reverie the person is fully aware of what is taking place in the present.
3. **narco:** short for narcosynthesis. See **narcosynthesis** in the glossary.
4. **charge:** suffusion, as with emotion, such as hopelessness.

That's *valence*.[5] An aberree has a valence for every person in every engram. He has basically three, himself, Mother and Father. Every engram has dramatic personnel. A valence builds up in the reactive mind and walls off a compartment, absorbing some of the analyzer—which is shut down by restimulation. Multivalence is common to every aberree. The valence of every aberree gets shifted day to day depending upon whom he meets. He tries to occupy the top-dog valence in every engramic dramatization. Taking this is the highest survival computation that can be made by the reactive mind; always win. Break a dramatization and you break the patient into another valence. If you break him down to being himself in that engram he will probably go anaten or get sick. Keep breaking his dramatizations and he is disabled mentally.

Who will practice Dianetics? In severe cases, doctors. They are well schooled in the art of healing, they are always being bombarded by psychosomatics and mental situations. The doctor has, like the engineer, a certain necessity for results. There are several methods of alleviation which can work in as little as a few hours to help break up a chronic illness in a child, change valences, change a person's position on the time track—people get caught in various places where the command says to be caught—alter dramatization pattern and generally assist the sick aberree.

In the general case, however—the psychotic, neurotic, or merely suboptimum individual—Dianetics will probably be practiced by people of intelligence and good drive on their friends and families. Knowing all the axioms and mechanisms, Dianetics is easy to apply to the fairly normal individual and can relieve his occlusions and colds and arthritis and other psychosomatic ills. It can be used as well to prevent aberrations

---

5. **valence:** literally, the word means the ability to combine with or take on parts of another. In Dianetics, *valence* is an actual or shadow personality. One's own valence is his actual personality. A shadow personality is the taking on of the physical and/or emotional characteristics or traits of another. *Multivalence* would be *many personalities.*

from occurring and can even be applied to determine the reactions of others. Although the fundamentals and mechanisms are simple and, with some study, very easily applied, partial information is dangerous. The technique may be the stuff of which sanity is made, but one is after all engaging action with the very stuff which creates madness and he should at least inform himself with a few hours' study before he experiments.

~≈~

CHAPTER TWELVE

THE HOPE FOR
THE FUTURE

THE HOPE FOR THE FUTURE

I HAVE DISCUSSED HERE THE evolution of Dianetics. Actually I have concentrated upon Abnormal Dianetics. There are Medical Dianetics, Dynamic Dianetics (drives and structure), Political Dianetics, Military Dianetics, Industrial Dianetics, et cetera, et cetera, and not the least, PREVENTIVE DIANETICS. On that may hang the final answer to society.*

And now as an epilogue, Dianetics is summarized in its current workable form. It does the following things, based on an ample series of cases:

1. Dianetics is an organized science of thought built on definite axioms; it apparently reveals the existence of natural laws by which behavior can uniformly be caused or predicted in the unit organism or society.

2. Dianetics offers a therapeutic technique with which we can treat any and all inorganic mental and organic psychosomatic ills. It produces a mental stability in the "cleared" patient which is far superior to the current norm. (This statement is accurate to date; it is conceded that further work may demonstrate some particular case somewhere, which may not entirely respond.)

*See the book *Dianetics: The Modern Science of Mental Health* by L. Ron Hubbard.

3. In Dianetics we have a method of time dislocation, dissimilar to narcosynthesis or hypnosis, which is called the Dianetic reverie; with it the patient is able to reach events hitherto hidden from him, erasing the physical and mental pain from his life.

4. Dianetics gives us an insight into the potential capabilities of the mind.

5. Dianetics reveals the basic nature of man and his purposes and intents, with the discovery that these are basically constructive and not evil.

6. Dianetics gives us an appreciation of the magnitude of events necessary to aberrate an individual.

7. With Dianetics we discover the nature of prenatal experience and its precise effect upon the postnatal individual.

8. Dianetics discovered the actual aberrative factors of birth.

9. Dianetics elucidates the entire problem of "unconsciousness" and demonstrates conclusively that "total unconsciousness" does not exist short of death.

10. Dianetics shows that all memories of all kinds are recorded fully and retained.

11. Dianetics demonstrates that aberrative memories lie only in areas of "unconsciousness" and, conversely, that only "unconscious" memories are capable of aberrating.

12. Dianetics opens broad avenues for research and poses numerous problems for solution. One new field, for instance, is

the subscience of perceptics—the structure and function of perceiving and identifying stimuli.

13. Dianetics sets forth the nongerm theory of disease, embracing, it has been estimated by competent physicians, the explanation of some seventy percent of man's pathology.

14. Dianetics offers hope that the destruction of the function of the brain, by shock or surgery, will no longer be a necessary evil.

15. Dianetics offers a workable explanation of the various physiological effects of drugs and endocrine substances and points out numerous answers to former endocrine problems.

16. Dianetics gives a more fundamental explanation of the uses, principles and fundamentals of hypnotism and similar mental phenomena.

17. To sum up, Dianetics proposes and experimentally supports a new viewpoint on man and his behavior. It carries with it the necessity of a new sort of mental hygiene. It indicates a new method of approach to the solution of the problems which confront governments, social agencies, industries, and, in short, man's sphere of endeavor. It suggests new fields of research. Finally it offers a glimmer of hope that Man may continue his process of evolution toward a higher organism without straying toward the danger point of his own destruction.

This is part of the story of the search. I wrote it for you this way because you have minds with which to think. For strictly professional publications, I can, will and have dressed this up so it's exact. A lot of you have been reading my stories for years.

"Up there are the stars. Down in the arsenal is an atom bomb. Which one is it going to be?"

We know each other. Here, I have told you the story as is and I have given you the major results exactly as they turned out.

The black enchantment of Earth didn't turn out to be a sinister barrier. But it's a black enchantment all the same. The social and personal aberrations, traveling from Egypt's time and before, piling up higher and higher, being broken only by new lands and new mongrel races.

The black enchantment is slavery. Man's effort to enslave man so that man can be free. Wrong equation. That's the black enchantment. We've a magic word to break it and a science to be applied.

Up there are the stars. Down in the arsenal is an atom bomb.

Which one is it going to be?

ABOUT
L. RON HUBBARD

L. RON HUBBARD IS BROADLY acclaimed as one of the twentieth century's most influential authors, with more than 160 million copies of his works in worldwide circulation. As the founder of Dianetics and Scientology, his philosophic breakthroughs have helped people all over the world to better understand themselves and others.

"To know life," he once wrote, "you've got to be part of life. You must get down there and look, you must get into the nooks and crannies of existence, and you must rub elbows with all kinds and types of men before you can finally establish what man is."

Through a long and adventurous pursuit of knowledge, L. Ron Hubbard did just that.

His abiding interest in the human mind was initially sparked when, at the age of twelve, he studied under Commander Joseph C. Thompson—an early student of psychoanalysis and the first United States naval officer to study with Freud in Vienna. Although Ron would ultimately reject Freudian theory as both impractical and unworkable, he nonetheless came to one pivotal conclusion: "Something can be done about the mind."

Pursuing his search across the South Pacific to Asia, Ron became one of the few Americans admitted into holy Tibetan lamaseries in the Western Hills of China. He additionally studied with the last in line of royal magicians from the court of Kublai Khan. Yet despite all the fabled wisdom of the East, he found lands of aching poverty and abject despair, and could only conclude: "Learning locked in mildewed books is of little use to anyone and therefore of no value unless it can be used."

Returning to the United States, Ron next pursued a course of study in engineering, mathematics and nuclear physics at George Washington University, all disciplines that would serve him well through his later philosophic inquiry. In point of fact, L. Ron Hubbard was the first to rigorously employ Western empirical methods to the study of the mind and spirit, beginning with his university research into subjects as diverse as human memory storage and the nature of aesthetics. Yet beyond a basic methodology and thus a yardstick for further inquiry, university offered no real answers.

Indeed, as he later wrote, "It was very obvious that I was dealing with and living in a culture which knew less about the mind than the lowest primitive tribe I had ever come in contact with." Consequently, he added, "I knew I would have to do a lot of research."

That research consumed the next several decades, and his laboratory was the world. Without access to comfortable "research grants," and supported only by his acclaimed literary career, Ron studied no less than 21 primitive races and cultures—from Pacific Northwest Indian tribes and Philippine Tagalogs to the Puerto Rican hill people. (In consequence, he is also remembered today on the rosters of the prestigious New York Explorers Club.)

The Second World War proved both an interruption of research and a further impetus to develop an actual technology of the human mind. The first procedures were tested at Oak Knoll Naval Hospital in Northern California where a then-Lieutenant L. Ron Hubbard received treatment for wounds suffered in combat. His research cases were former prisoners of Japanese internment camps—men whom medical science had all but given up. Yet with the employment of seminal Dianetics techniques, each and every one of those Ron treated, summarily and quite remarkably, regained health.

With the restoration of peace, Ron set out to further test the workability of Dianetics, and with individuals from all walks of life. In full, to develop Dianetics as a uniquely practical and effective technology, he tested procedures on hundreds.

In 1947, he collected notes drawn from hundreds of case histories amassed through preceding years of testing, and prepared a thesis detailing both underlying theory and techniques. Copies of the manuscript were distributed to medical and scientific circles, then eagerly recopied and passed to friends. In that way, Ron's original thesis on Dianetics saw immediate and wide circulation. Today, that thesis is published as *The Dynamics of Life*. The work was followed, in late 1949, with an article written expressly for *The Explorers Journal* entitled "Terra Incognita: The Mind."

To meet the veritable flood of inquiries from readers, Ron was next urged to author a definitive text on the subject. Accordingly, in early 1950, he began work on *Dianetics: The Modern Science of Mental Health*. Concurrently, by way of a broad public introduction to Dianetics, and as a prelude to publication, Ron further authored a book-length article for a national American magazine. That article, detailing his developmental trail and providing an overview of universal application, was *Dianetics: The Evolution of a Science*. It appeared on newsstands in April of 1950, and was promptly read by virtually every leading engineer and physicist. To be sure, *Dianetics: The Evolution of a Science* effectively galvanized the whole of a United States scientific community.

The subsequent release of *Dianetics: The Modern Science of Mental Health* became a landmark event in publishing history, capturing wide public interest and acclaim. The work immediately topped the *New York Times* bestseller list and remained there week after week. It has since become the most widely read and used book on the human mind in history, with nearly 20 million copies in circulation.

Today, Dianetics is a worldwide phenomenon, used by millions in more than 150 nations and in over 50 languages.

L. Ron Hubbard's works on the subject of man, the mind and spirit today comprise tens of millions of published words recorded in volumes of books, manuscripts and over 3,000 recorded lectures.

The greatest testimonies to Ron's vision are the miracle results of his technology, and the millions of friends around the world who carry his legacy forward into the twenty-first century. Both continue to grow in number with each passing day.

"I like to help others," he once said, "and count it as my greatest pleasure in life to see a person free himself of the shadows which darken his days.

"These shadows look so thick to him and weigh him down so that when he finds they are shadows and that he can see through them, walk through them and be again in the sun, he is enormously delighted. And I am afraid I am just as delighted as he is."

"I AM ALWAYS HAPPY TO HEAR FROM MY READERS."

L. RON HUBBARD

THESE WERE THE WORDS of L. Ron Hubbard, who was always very interested in hearing from his friends and readers. He made a point of staying in communication with everyone he came in contact with over his more than fifty-year career as a professional writer, and he had thousands of fans and friends that he corresponded with all over the world.

The author's representatives, Author Services, Inc., wish to continue this tradition and welcome letters and comments from you, his readers, both old and new.

Additionally, they will be happy to send you information on anything you would like to know about L. Ron Hubbard, his extraordinary life and accomplishments and the vast number of books he has written.

Any message addressed to the Author's Affairs Director at Author Services, Inc., will be given prompt and full attention.

AUTHOR SERVICES, INC.

7051 HOLLYWOOD BOULEVARD, HOLLYWOOD, CALIFORNIA 90028, USA

authoraffairs@authorservicesinc.com

GLOSSARY

A

aberrated: affected by *aberration:* a departure from rational thought or behavior; not sane. From the Latin, *aberrare,* to wander from; *ab,* away, *errare,* to wander. Chapter 2, #3

aberree: an aberrated person. Chapter 4, #3

Adler: See **Freud, Jung, Adler** in this glossary.

amnesia trance: a deep trance of a person in a sleep, making him susceptible to commands. Chapter 3, #5

analog: something having analogy to something else. An analogy is a similarity between like features of two things on which a comparison may be based. Chapter 7, #3

arbitrary: something derived from mere opinion; something unreasonable or unsupported. Chapter 5, #8

attenuation: the weakening or reduction in force, intensity, effect, quantity, or value. Chapter 9, #7

automatic writing: writing performed by a person without his conscious intention or awareness often encouraged in order to make contact with the writer's unconscious, uncovering censored or hidden data. Chapter 8, #1

axiom: a self-evident truth that requires no proof. Chapter 2, #2

B

back-seat driving: interfering in affairs from a subordinate position, giving unsolicited advice. From the practice of an automobile passenger offering a driver unsolicited advice, warnings, criticism, etc., especially from the back seat. Chapter 9, #19

bank: a storage of information, as in a computer where the data was once stored on a group or series of cards called a bank. Chapter 1, #1

banner and crescent: a reference to the flag and crescent symbol of Muslim armies which, during the Middle Ages, conquered much of Europe. Chapter 3, #10

Bedlam: an old insane asylum (in full, *St. Mary of Bethlehem*) in London, known for its inhumane treatment of its inmates. Chapter 3, #8

black enchantment: an evil or wicked spell. Chapter 4, #4

by-your-leave: an apology for not having sought permission. Chapter 9, #13

C

caliper: a precise measuring instrument having two curved legs or jaws that can be adjusted to determine thickness, diameter and distance between surfaces. Chapter 2, #16

Cap Haitien: a seaport on the north coast of Haiti. Chapter 6

Cathedral at Reims: a famous Gothic cathedral and chief landmark of the city of Reims in northeastern France. Chapter 2

Censor: (in early Freudian dream theory) the force that represses ideas, impulses, and feelings, and prevents them from entering consciousness in their original, undisguised forms. Chapter 8, #4

charge: suffusion, as with emotion, such as hopelessness. Chapter 11, #4

clairvoyance: keenness of mental perception, clearness of insight; insight into things beyond the image of ordinary perception. Chapter 8, #2

coefficient of expansion: in physics, a change in volume, area or length of a material that accompanies a change in temperature. For example, in a traditional thermometer, the volume of liquid mercury expands or contracts as it is heated or cooled by temperature. The amount of mercury expansion or contraction determines how high or low the thermometer reads. Chapter 7, #4

constant: something that does not or cannot change or vary. Chapter 2, #15

D

dermatitis: inflammation of the skin resulting in redness, swelling, itching or other symptoms. Chapter 9, #11

Dianetics: *Dianetics* means "through the mind" or "through the soul" (from Greek *dia*, "through" and *nous*, "mind" or "soul"). It is a system of coordinated axioms which resolve problems concerning human behavior and psychosomatic illnesses. It combines a workable technique and a thoroughly validated method for increasing sanity, by erasing unwanted sensations and unpleasant emotions.

disputative: inclined to argue; quarrelsome. Chapter 2, #13

dope: *(slang)* information, data, or news. *Hot dope* would be very exciting or interesting information. Chapter 10, #7

dynamic: active, energetic, effective, forceful, motivating, as opposed to static. Chapter 2, #11

dynamo: a machine that generates electricity. Chapter 2, #10

E

ectoplasm: in spiritualism, the vaporous, luminous substance, which is supposed to emanate from a medium during a trance. Chapter 4, #5

elucidate: to make clear, explain. Chapter 12

encephalograph: an instrument for measuring and recording the electric activity of the brain. Chapter 7, #5

endocrine: having to do with the secretion of hormones (chemical substances) from certain organs and tissues in the body. Some of these organs increase blood pressure and heart rate during times of stress. Chapter 9, #9

equivocal: of doubtful nature or character; questionable; dubious; suspicious. Chapter 8, #3

ether: a colorless liquid, having an aromatic odor and sweet, burning taste, used formerly as an inhalant anesthetic. Chapter 9, #1

exorcist: one who drives out evil spirits (from a person or place) by religious or solemn ceremony. Chapter 3, #1

F

fold up: to break down, collapse; to fail. Chapter 8, #5

force: persuasive power; power to convince. Chapter 8, #12

Freud, Jung, Adler: psychologists Sigmund Freud (1856–1939), Carl Gustav Jung (1875–1961) and Alfred Adler (1870–1937). Freud founded psychoanalysis and while Jung and Adler collaborated with him at first, both parted company and founded their independent schools of thought as they disagreed with Freud's emphasis on sex as a driving force. Jung theorized that all humans inherit a *collective unconscious*, which contains universal symbols and memories from their ancestral past, while Adler thought people were primarily motivated to overcome inherent feelings of inferiority. Chapter 5, #2

fuse: *(figurative)* to install a device to protect against shock, overload, etc. From the field of electricity where in an electric circuit, a strip of easily melting metal is inserted, which melts (or "blows") and thus interrupts the electrical flow to prevent damage should the electrical current increase beyond a certain safe level. Chapter 9, #3

G

general semantics: a highly organized philosophical approach to language, developed by Alfred Korzybski (1879–1950), which sought a scientific basis for a clear understanding of the difference between words and reality and the ways in which words themselves can influence and limit man's ability to think. Chapter 9, #8

Goldberg, Rube: (1883–1970) American cartoonist known for his depiction of ridiculously intricate mechanical devices designed to accomplish absurdly simple tasks. Chapter 6, #3

Goldi: a people, traditionally hunters and fishermen in southeastern Siberia and northeastern Manchuria. Chapter 2

H

hark back: to return or revert to some earlier point. Chapter 3, #11

heuristic: using experimentation, evaluation, or trial-and-error methods. Chapter 6

heuristically: characterized by the use of experimentation, evaluation or trial-and-error methods. Chapter 2, #1

hooker: a concealed problem, flaw, or drawback; a catch. Chapter 5, #9

hypnoanalysis: a method of psychoanalysis in which a patient is hypnotized in an attempt to reach analytic data and early emotional reactions. Chapter 3, #6

I

"I": (in philosophy and other fields) the source of thinking; the person himself, as distinct from the body, who is aware of being self; the soul. Chapter 7, #8

identity(ies): exact sameness in qualities or characteristics; equivalent or equal. (See Chapter 9 for description of *identity-thinking.*) Chapter 9, #4

imbibe: to take or receive into the mind, as knowledge, ideas, or the like. Chapter 5, #7

impedance: the preventing of progress; hindrance or something that delays or prevents progress. Chapter 9, #16

Indian rope trick: a magic trick, Oriental in origin, in which a magician suspends a rope in midair which a person then climbs up and seemingly disappears. Chapter 2, #14

interpose: to assume an intervening position; to come between other things. Chapter 8

interposition: something that assumes an intervening position; something that comes between two or more things. Chapter 8, #13

IQ: Intelligence Quotient, a number arrived at by means of intelligence tests and intended to indicate a person's intelligence. Chapter 10, #5

J

Jung: See **Freud, Jung, Adler** in this glossary.

K

Kant: Immanuel Kant (1724–1804), German philosopher who maintained that objects of experience (phenomena) may be known, but that things lying beyond the realm of possible experience are unknowable. Kant's works are often considered difficult to understand. Chapter 5, #1

Kayan: people native to the island of Borneo. Settled mainly on the Kayan River, they worship many gods and practice shamanism. Chapter 3, #12

keyed in: literally, a key is a small manual device for opening, closing or switching electronic contacts. *Key-in* is used here to describe a dormant engram that has activated and is now thrown into circuit. Chapter 9, #10

Khan, Kublai: (1216–1294) the grandson of the founder of the Mongol dynasty, Genghis Khan, and who completed the conquest of China begun by his grandfather. Chapter 2, #5

L

lock: a situation of mental anguish. It depends for its force on the engram to which it is appended. The lock is more or less known to the analyzer. It's a moment of severe restimulation of an engram. Chapter 9, #6

Lucretius: (ca. 98–55 B.C.) Roman poet who was the author of the unfinished instructional poem in six books, *On the Nature of Things,* which set forth in outline a complete science of the universe. Chapter 2, #19

M

main: sheer, utmost. Chapter 8, #11

Maxwell, Clerk: James Clerk Maxwell (1831–1879), Scottish physicist who, in order to graphically explain certain physical universe phenomena, invented a hypothetical creature (or demon) that he said controlled the motion of individual molecules of gas and caused them to act in specific ways he had observed. Chapter 2, #9

mensuration: the action of measuring. Chapter 2, #17

Mex: a half quantity of anything. Chapter 8, #6

monocycle: a vehicle with one wheel. Chapter 8, #7

N

narco: short for narcosynthesis. See **narcosynthesis** below. Chapter 11, #3

narcosynthesis: drug hypnotism whereby a patient undergoes psychotherapy while drugged and in a "deep sleep." Chapter 2, #8

necessity level: the degree to which an individual feels the need or necessity to take a certain course of action. Chapter 9, #17

needle-in-the-haystacking: from the expression "needle in the haystack" which refers to attempting to find a needle in a stack of hay—an extremely difficult or impossible task. Chapter 5, #6

neuron: a cell that transmits nerve impulses and is the basic functional unit of the nervous system; also called nerve cell. Chapter 7, #2

nitrous oxide: a sweet-smelling, sweet-tasting gas used in dentistry and surgery to render the patient unconscious. Chapter 5, #10

O

old-line Hindu principle: reference to the regression and revivification techniques used in Asia for thousands of years. Unlike recent Western schools, which held regression to be possible only in tranced or hypnotized subjects, in Asia this ability was found to be inherent in the fully alert individual. Chapter 8, #10

P

Pavlov: Ivan Petrovich Pavlov (1849–1936), Russian physiologist, noted for his dog experiments. Pavlov presented food to a dog, while he sounded a bell. After repeating this procedure several times, the dog (in anticipation) would salivate at the sound of the bell, whether or not food was presented. Pavlov concluded that all acquired habits, even the higher mental activity of man, depended on conditioned reflexes. Chapter 5, #3

perceptic: a perceived and recorded sense message, such as organic sensation, smell, taste, tactile, audio, visio, etc. Chapter 8

polarity: that quality or condition in a physical body or system that manifests opposite or contrasting properties, as in a magnet where one end is positive and the other negative. Reverse polarity refers to a state whereby two objects, conditions, etc., have opposing forces. Chapter 10, #2

posthypnotic suggestion: a suggestion made during hypnosis so as to be effective after awakening. Chapter 3, #4

postulate: a proposition that requires no proof, being self-evident, or that is for a specific purpose assumed true. Chapter 3, #13

postulating: assuming to be true, real or necessary, especially as a basis for reasoning. Chapter 2, #7

prefrontal lobotomy: a psychiatric operation carried out by boring holes into the skull, entering the brain and severing the nerve pathways in the two frontal lobes, resulting in the patient becoming an emotional vegetable. Chapter 3, #9

Prime Mover Unmoved: according to the philosophy of Aristotle (384–322 B.C.), that which is the first cause of all motion in the universe, which itself does not move. The Prime Mover was said to be eternal, immaterial and unchangeable, and Aristotle considered the Prime Mover as divine thought, mind or God. Chapter 2, #12

psychosomatics: body sensations, pains or discomfort stemming from the mind. Comes from *psycho* (mind) and *somatic* (body). Chapter 10, #4

push-button: stimulus-response. From the action of pushing a button which mechanically and predictably opens or closes an electrical circuit; for example, a doorbell. Chapter 9, #2

R

radical: a fundamental thing or character, basic principle. Chapter 3, #3

record: a reference to a phonograph record which consists of a disk with grooves in it. Chapter 9, #20

red-tab: to use a red tab so as to identify or earmark for a specific purpose, the color red often being associated with urgent or emergency situations, usually as a warning. Chapter 5, #5

reduce: to bring into a certain order; systematize. Chapter 1, #4

regression: a technique by which part of the individual's self remained in the present and part went back to the past. Chapter 8, #8

restimulation: a condition in which an approximation of the reactive mind's content or some part thereof is perceived in the environment of the organism. Chapter 9, #5

restimulator: the environment's equivalent to the engram's perceptic content. Chapter 10

reverie: a light state of "concentration" not to be confused with hypnosis; in reverie the person is fully aware of what is taking place in the present. Chapter 11, #2

revivification: the reliving of an incident or some portion of it as if it were happening now. Chapter 8, #9

S

Salinas Valley: a fertile valley located in western California south of San Francisco, USA, through which runs the Salinas River. Chapter 2

savant: a person of extensive learning. Chapter 4, #1

schizophrenic: a person with two (or more) apparent personalities. *Schizophrenia* means *scissors* or *two*, plus *head*. Literally, *splitting of the mind*, hence, *split personality*. Chapter 4, #2

Scientology: *Dianetics* was the forerunner of Scientology. By use of Dianetics it became apparent that it dealt, not with cells and cellular memory, but with a human spirit that defied time. Scientology addresses the world of thought, of life itself. Its target is spiritual freedom and ability. The term is taken from the Latin word *scio* (knowing in the fullest sense of the word), and the Greek word *logos* (study of). In itself the word means literally *knowing how to know*. It is further defined as *the study and handling of the spirit in relationship to itself, universes and other life.*

seat: a place in which something occurs or is established; physical location. Chapter 9, #18

sentient: conscious or capable of perceptions; consciously perceiving. Chapter 7, #1

seven-league-boot stride: *(figurative)* an enormous leap in progress, significant forward motion, as if one had taken a step that was seven leagues. Such boots are found in a fairy tale allowing one to cover seven leagues (about 21 miles or 34 kilometers) in a single step. Chapter 6, #5

shaman: a priest or priestess who is said to act as an intermediary between natural and supernatural worlds and to use magic to cure ailments, foretell the future and to contact and control spiritual forces. Chapter 2, #4

Shannon: Dr. Claude E. Shannon (1916–), US mathematician whose work impacted upon the development of computer and communications technology. Chapter 7, #7

somatics: physical pain, discomfort, unwanted emotions or feelings coming from an engram. Chapter 10, #6

Spencer: Herbert Spencer (1820–1903), English philosopher known for his application of the scientific doctrines of evolution to philosophy and ethics. Chapter 2, #18

stet: "let it stand," a printer's term used to indicate that matter previously marked for deletion is to remain. Chapter 6, #2

stupefaction: a dazed or dull condition, where perception and understanding are blunted or deadened. Chapter 9, #12

surcharge: an additional or excessive load or burden. Chapter 10, #3

symbiotes: organisms, persons, groups, etc., living in an inter-dependent or mutually beneficial relationship. The atom depends on the universe, the universe on the atom. Chapter 10, #1

T

tactile: the sense of touch. Chapter 1, #3

Tarawa: an island in the central Pacific Ocean captured from the Japanese by US Marines in 1943, after very heavy fighting. Chapter 6, #1

10^{21} **binary digits:** *binary* comes from a Latin word meaning *two at a time. Binary digits* refers to a system of numbering employed in computers which use only two numbers (digits), 0 and 1. 10^{21} *binary digits* refers to an enormous quantity of 0s and 1s (1,000,000,000,000,000,000,000 of them) strung out one after another, forming a huge number. Chapter 2, #6

Toh: an agent of the spiritual world in primitive cultures. *Toh* are considered malevolent spirits and are blamed for disasters, such as crop failures, sickness and death. Chapter 3, #14

U

UNIVAC: (late 1940s to late 1950s) *Universal Automatic Computer:* the first electronic computer designed and sold to solve commercial problems. Chapter 6, #4

U

vacuum-tube rig: a reference to computers as they existed in the late 1940s. The vacuum tube was a device broadly used in electronics to control flows of electrical currents. It is called a vacuum tube because it is a sealed glass tube or bulb from which almost all the air had been removed in order to improve electrical flow. Chapter 7, #6

valence: literally, the word means the ability to combine with or take on parts of another. In Dianetics, *valence* is an actual or shadow personality. One's own valence is his actual personality. A shadow personality is the taking on of the physical and/or emotional characteristics or traits of another. *Multivalence* would be *many personalities.* Chapter 11, #5

visio: the sense of sight. Chapter 1, #2

vox populi: popular sentiment or the expressed general opinion. *Vox populi* is a Latin phrase which literally means "voice of the people." Chapter 11, #1

W

water cure: a psychiatric treatment, purported to remove demons from a person whereby the patient was stretched out on the ground and had water poured into his mouth from some height. Chapter 3, #7

Western Hills: a range of hills in China, situated northwest of the Chinese capital, Beijing. The range is known for its many temples and has long been a religious retreat. Chapter 6

what price: an expression or concept meaning "so much for"; what is the value of ——— ? Chapter 9, #14

Whoosis: an indefinite or unspecified person or thing or one that is representative or typical. Chapter 5, #4

wild: unrestricted, uncontrolled, erratic, unsteady. Chapter 3, #2

willy-nilly: whether one wishes to or not; willingly or unwillingly. Chapter 9, #15

INDEX

INDEX

—O🔑—

WHERE TO GO
FOR DIANETICS
TRAINING AND
AUDITING

LEARN HOW TO USE DIANETICS
AND ACHIEVE THE STATE OF CLEAR

A Clear has no vicious reactive mind and operates at full mental capacity. YOU can reach the State of Clear just as many thousands have before you.

Start on your road to Clear on the Hubbard Dianetics Seminar. Learn to apply the proven techniques of Dianetics with confidence and certainty. Work with other students, under trained supervision, both giving and receiving auditing, and experience the life changing miracles of Dianetics for yourself.

Contact your nearest Hubbard Dianetics Foundation and enroll on the Hubbard Dianetics Seminar. There are thousands of Dianetics groups and organizations all over the world. Below are the organizations in the United States, Canada, United Kingdom, Australia and Africa. To find other Hubbard Dianetics Foundations internationally, visit the Dianetics website at **www.dianetics.org** and use the Global Locator.

Or call or write to the publisher, who will direct you to your nearest Hubbard Dianetics Foundation:

WESTERN HEMISPHERE: EASTERN HEMISPHERE:

Bridge Publications, Inc.   New Era Publications
4751 Fountain Avenue   International ApS
Los Angeles, California   Store Kongensgade 53
90029   1264 Copenhagen K, Denmark
1-800-722-1733   (45) 33 73 66 66

UNITED STATES

ALBUQUERQUE

Hubbard Dianetics
Foundation
8106 Menaul Boulevard NE
Albuquerque, New Mexico
87110

ANN ARBOR

Hubbard Dianetics
Foundation
66 E. Michigan Avenue
Battle Creek, Michigan 49017

ATLANTA

Hubbard Dianetics
Foundation
1611 Mt. Vernon Road
Dunwoody, Georgia 30338

AUSTIN

Hubbard Dianetics
Foundation
2200 Guadalupe
Austin, Texas 78705

BOSTON

Hubbard Dianetics
Foundation
448 Beacon Street
Boston, Massachusetts 02115

BUFFALO

Hubbard Dianetics
Foundation
47 West Huron Street
Buffalo, New York 14202

CHICAGO

Hubbard Dianetics
Foundation
3011 North Lincoln Avenue
Chicago, Illinois 60657-4207

CINCINNATI

Hubbard Dianetics
Foundation
215 West 4th Street,
5th Floor
Cincinnati, Ohio 45202-2670

CLEARWATER

Flag Service Organization
210 S. Fort Harrison Avenue
Clearwater, Florida 33756

Flag Ship Service
Organization
c/o *Freewinds* Relay Office
118 N. Fort Harrison Avenue
Clearwater, Florida
33755-4013

COLUMBUS

Hubbard Dianetics
Foundation
30 North High Street
Columbus, Ohio 43215

DALLAS

Celebrity Centre Dallas
1850 North Buckner
Boulevard
Dallas, Texas 75228

Denver

Hubbard Dianetics
Foundation
3385 South Bannock Street
Englewood, Colorado 80110

Detroit

Hubbard Dianetics
Foundation
28000 Middlebelt Road
Farmington Hills, Michigan
48334

Honolulu

Hubbard Dianetics
Foundation
1146 Bethel Street
Honolulu, Hawaii 96813

Kansas City

Hubbard Dianetics
Foundation
2 East 39th Street
Kansas City, Missouri 64111

Las Vegas

Hubbard Dianetics
Foundation
846 East Sahara Avenue
Las Vegas, Nevada 89104

Celebrity Centre Las Vegas
4850 W. Flamingo Road,
Suite 10
Las Vegas, Nevada 89103

Long Island

Hubbard Dianetics
Foundation
99 Railroad Station Plaza
Hicksville, New York
11801-2850

Los Angeles
AND VICINITY

Hubbard Dianetics
Foundation
4810 Sunset Boulevard
Los Angeles, California 90027

Hubbard Dianetics
Foundation
1451 Irvine Boulevard
Tustin, California 92680

Hubbard Dianetics
Foundation
1277 East Colorado Boulevard
Pasadena, California 91106

Hubbard Dianetics
Foundation
15643 Sherman Way
Van Nuys, California 91406

American Saint Hill
Organization
1413 L. Ron Hubbard Way
Los Angeles, California 90027

American Saint Hill
Foundation
1413 L. Ron Hubbard Way
Los Angeles, California 90027

Advanced Organization
of Los Angeles
1306 L. Ron Hubbard Way
Los Angeles, California 90027

Celebrity Centre
International
5930 Franklin Avenue
Hollywood, California 90028

LOS GATOS

Hubbard Dianetics
Foundation
2155 South Bascom Avenue,
Suite 120
Campbell, California 95008

MIAMI

Hubbard Dianetics
Foundation
120 Giralda Avenue
Coral Gables, Florida 33134

MINNEAPOLIS

Hubbard Dianetics
Foundation
Twin Cities
1011 Nicollet Mall
Minneapolis, Minnesota
55403

MOUNTAIN VIEW

Hubbard Dianetics
Foundation
117 Easy Street
Mountain View, California
94039

NASHVILLE

Celebrity Centre Nashville
1204 16th Avenue South
Nashville, Tennessee 37212

NEW HAVEN

Hubbard Dianetics
Foundation
909 Whalley Avenue
New Haven, Connecticut
06515-1728

NEW YORK CITY

Hubbard Dianetics
Foundation
227 West 46th Street
New York, New York
10036-1409

Celebrity Centre New York
65 East 82nd Street
New York, New York 10028

ORLANDO

Hubbard Dianetics
Foundation
1830 East Colonial Drive
Orlando, Florida 32803-4729

PHILADELPHIA

Hubbard Dianetics
Foundation
1315 Race Street
Philadelphia, Pennsylvania
19107

PHOENIX

Hubbard Dianetics
Foundation
2111 West University Drive
Mesa, Arizona 85201

PORTLAND

Hubbard Dianetics
Foundation
2636 NE Sandy Boulevard
Portland, Oregon 97232-2342

Celebrity Centre Portland
708 SW Salmon Street
Portland, Oregon 97205

SACRAMENTO

Hubbard Dianetics
Foundation
825 15th Street
Sacramento, California
95814-2096

SALT LAKE CITY

Hubbard Dianetics
Foundation
1931 South 1100 East
Salt Lake City, Utah 84106

SAN DIEGO

Hubbard Dianetics
Foundation
1330 4th Avenue
San Diego, California 92101

SAN FRANCISCO

Hubbard Dianetics
Foundation
83 McAllister Street
San Francisco, California
94102

SAN JOSE

Hubbard Dianetics
Foundation
80 East Rosemary Street
San Jose, California 95112

SANTA BARBARA

Hubbard Dianetics
Foundation
524 State Street
Santa Barbara, California
93101

SEATTLE

Hubbard Dianetics
Foundation
2226 3rd Avenue
Seattle, Washington 98121

ST. LOUIS

Hubbard Dianetics
Foundation
6901 Delmar Boulevard
University City, Missouri
63130

TAMPA

Hubbard Dianetics
Foundation
3617 Henderson Boulevard
Tampa, Florida 33609-4501

WASHINGTON, DC

Hubbard Dianetics
Foundation
1701 20th Street NW
Washington, DC 20009

PUERTO RICO

HATO REY

Dianetics Center of
Puerto Rico
272 JT Piñero Avenue
Hyde Park
San Juan, Puerto Rico 00918

CANADA

EDMONTON

Hubbard Dianetics
Foundation
10255 97th Street
Edmonton, Alberta
Canada T5J 0L9

KITCHENER

Hubbard Dianetics
Foundation
159–161 King Street West
Kitchener, Ontario
Canada N2G 1A6

MONTREAL

Hubbard Dianetics
Foundation
4489 Papineau Street
Montreal, Quebec
Canada H2H 1T7

OTTAWA

Hubbard Dianetics
Foundation
150 Rideau Street, 2nd Floor
Ottawa, Ontario
Canada K1N 5X6

QUEBEC

Hubbard Dianetics
Foundation
350 Bd Chareste Est
Quebec, Quebec
Canada G1K 3H5

TORONTO

Hubbard Dianetics
Foundation
696 Yonge Street, 2nd Floor
Toronto, Ontario
Canada M4Y 2A7

VANCOUVER

Hubbard Dianetics
Foundation
401 West Hastings Street
Vancouver, British Columbia
Canada V6B 1L5

WINNIPEG

Hubbard Dianetics
Foundation
315 Garry Street, Suite 210
Winnipeg, Manitoba
Canada R3B 2G7

LATIN AMERICA

ARGENTINA

BUENOS AIRES

Dianetics Association of
Argentina
2162 Bartolomé Mitre
Capital Federal
Buenos Aires 1039, Argentina

COLOMBIA

BOGOTÁ

Dianetics Cultural Center
Carrera 30 #91–96
Bogotá, Colombia

MEXICO

GUADALAJARA

Dianetics Cultural
 Organization, A.C.
Avenida de la Paz 2787
Fracc. Arcos Sur
Sector Juárez, Guadalajara,
Jalisco
CP 44500, Mexico

MEXICO CITY

Dianetics Cultural
 Association, A.C.
Belisario Domínguez #17-1
Villa Coyoacán
Colonia Coyoacán
CP 04000, Mexico, D.F.

Institute of Applied
 Philosophy, A.C.
Municipio Libre No. 40
Esq. Mira Flores
Colonia Portales
Mexico, D.F.

Latin American Cultural
 Center, A.C.
Rio Amazonas 11
Colonia Cuahutemoc
CP 06500, Mexico, D.F.

Dianetics Technological
 Institute, A.C.
Avenida Chapultepec 540,
 6° Piso
Colonia Roma, Metro
 Chapultepec
CP 06700, Mexico, D.F.

Dianetics Development
 Organization, A.C.
Avenida Xola #1113 Esq.
 Pitágoras
Colonia Narvarte
CP 03220, Mexico, D.F.

Dianetics Cultural
 Organization, A.C.
Calle Monterrey #402
Colonia Narvarte
CP 03020, Mexico, D.F.

VENEZUELA

CARACAS

Dianetics Cultural
 Organization, A.C.
Calle Caciquiare
Entre Yumare y Atures
Quinta Shangai
Urbanización El Marquez
Caracas, Venezuela

VALENCIA

Dianetics Cultural
 Association, A.C.
Ave. Bolívar Norte
Urbanización el Viñedo
Edificio "Mi Refugio" #141-45
A 30 Metros de Ave Monseñor
 Adams
Valencia, Edo. Carabobo
Venezuela

UNITED KINGDOM

BIRMINGHAM

Hubbard Dianetics
 Foundation
8 Ethel Street
Winston Churchill House
Birmingham, England B2 4BG

BRIGHTON

Hubbard Dianetics
Foundation
Third Floor, 79-83 North
Street
Brighton, Sussex
England BN1 1ZA

EAST GRINSTEAD

Saint Hill Foundation
Saint Hill Manor
East Grinstead, West Sussex
England RH19 4JY

Advanced Organization
Saint Hill
Saint Hill Manor
East Grinstead, West Sussex
England RH19 4JY

EDINBURGH

Hubbard Academy of Personal
Independence
20 Southbridge
Edinburgh, Scotland EH1 1LL

LONDON

Hubbard Dianetics
Foundation
68 Tottenham Court Road
London, England W1P 0BB

Celebrity Centre London
42 Leinster Gardens
London, England W2 3AN

MANCHESTER

Hubbard Dianetics
Foundation
258 Deansgate
Manchester, England M3 4BG

PLYMOUTH

Hubbard Dianetics
Foundation
41 Ebrington Street
Plymouth, Devon
England PL4 9AA

SUNDERLAND

Hubbard Dianetics
Foundation
51 Fawcett Street
Sunderland, Tyne and Wear
England SR1 1RS

EUROPE

AUSTRIA

VIENNA

Hubbard Dianetics
Foundation
Schottenfeldgasse 13/15
1070 Vienna, Austria

Celebrity Centre Vienna
Senefeldergasse 11/5
1100 Vienna, Austria

BELGIUM

BRUSSELS

Hubbard Dianetics
Foundation
rue General MacArthur, 9
1180 Brussels, Belgium

DENMARK

AARHUS

Hubbard Dianetics
Foundation
Vester Alle 26
8000 Aarhus C, Denmark

COPENHAGEN

Hubbard Dianetics
Foundation
Store Kongensgade 55
1264 Copenhagen K
Denmark

Hubbard Dianetics
Foundation
Gammel Kongevej 3–5, 1
1610 Copenhagen V
Denmark

Advanced Organization
Saint Hill for Europe and
Africa
Jernbanegade 6
1608 Copenhagen V
Denmark

FRANCE

ANGERS

Hubbard Dianetics
Foundation
28B, avenue Mendès
49240 Avrille, France

CLERMONT-FERRAND

Hubbard Dianetics
Foundation
6, rue Dulaure
63000 Clermont-Ferrand
France

LYON

Hubbard Dianetics
Foundation
3, place des Capucins
69001 Lyon, France

PARIS

Hubbard Dianetics
Foundation
7, rue Jules César
75012 Paris, France

Celebrity Centre Paris
69, rue Legendre
75017 Paris, France

SAINT-ÉTIENNE

Hubbard Dianetics
Foundation
24, rue Marengo
42000 Saint-Étienne, France

GERMANY

BERLIN

Hubbard Dianetics
Foundation
Sponholzstraße 51–52
12159 Berlin 41
Germany

DÜSSELDORF

Hubbard Dianetics
Foundation
Friedrichstraße 28B
40217 Düsseldorf, Germany

Celebrity Centre Düsseldorf
Rheinland e. V.
Luisenstraße 23
40215 Düsseldorf, Germany

FRANKFURT

Hubbard Dianetics
Foundation
Kaiserstraße 49
60329 Frankfurt 70
Germany

HAMBURG

Hubbard Dianetics
Foundation
Domstraße 9
20095 Hamburg, Germany

Hubbard Dianetics
Foundation
Brennerstraße 12
20099 Hamburg, Germany

HANOVER

Hubbard Dianetics
Foundation
Odeonstraße 17
30159 Hanover, Germany

MUNICH

Hubbard Dianetics
Foundation
Beichstraße 12
80802 Munich 40
Germany

STUTTGART

Hubbard Dianetics
Foundation
Hohenheimerstraße 9
70184 Stuttgart, Germany

HUNGARY

BUDAPEST

Hubbard Dianetics
Foundation
1399 Budapest
1073 Erzsébet krt. 5. I. em.
Pf. 701/215. Hungary

ISRAEL

TEL AVIV

Hubbard Dianetics
Foundation
12 Shontzino Street
PO Box 57478
61573 Tel Aviv, Israel

ITALY

BRESCIA

Hubbard Dianetics
Foundation
Via Fratelli Bronzetti, 20
25125 Brescia, Italy

CATANIA

Hubbard Dianetics
Foundation
Via Garibaldi, 9
95121 Catania, Italy

MILAN

Hubbard Dianetics
Foundation
Via Lepontina, 4
20159 Milan, Italy

MONZA

Hubbard Dianetics
Foundation
Via Ghilini, 4
20052 Monza (MI), Italy

NOVARA

Hubbard Dianetics
Foundation
Corso Milano, 28
28100 Novara, Italy

NUORO

Hubbard Dianetics
Foundation
Via Lamarmora, 102
08100 Nuoro, Italy

PADUA

Hubbard Dianetics
Foundation
Via Ugo Foscolo, 5
35131 Padua, Italy

PORDENONE

Hubbard Dianetics
Foundation
Via Dogana, 19
Zona Fiera
33170 Pordenone, Italy

ROME

Hubbard Dianetics
Foundation
Via del Caravita, 5
00186 Rome, Italy

TURIN

Hubbard Dianetics
Foundation
Via Bersezio, 7
10152 Turin, Italy

VERONA

Hubbard Dianetics
Foundation
Corso Milano, 84
37138 Verona, Italy

NETHERLANDS

AMSTERDAM

Hubbard Dianetics
Foundation
Nieuwezijds Voorburgwal
116–118 1012 SH
Amsterdam, Netherlands

NORWAY

OSLO

Hubbard Dianetics
Foundation
Storgata 17
0184 Oslo, Norway

PORTUGAL

LISBON

Hubbard Dianetics
Foundation
Rua dos Correiros N 205,
3° Andar
1100 Lisbon, Portugal

RUSSIA

MOSCOW

Hubbard Humanitarian
Center
Ul. Boris Galushkina 19A
129301 Moscow, Russia

ST. PETERSBURG

Hubbard Dianetics
Foundation
Ligovskij Prospect 33
193036 St. Petersburg, Russia

SPAIN

BARCELONA

Dianetics Civil Association
Pasaje Domingo, 11–13 Bahos
08007 Barcelona, Spain

MADRID

Dianetics Civil Association
Villa Maria
C/ Montera 20, Piso 1º dcha.
28013 Madrid, Spain

SWEDEN

GÖTEBORG

Hubbard Dianetics
Foundation
Värmlandsgatan 16, 1 tr.
413 28 Göteborg, Sweden

MALMÖ

Hubbard Dianetics
Foundation
Porslinsgatan 3
211 32 Malmö, Sweden

STOCKHOLM

Hubbard Dianetics
Foundation
Götgatan 105
116 62 Stockholm, Sweden

SWITZERLAND

BASEL

Hubbard Dianetics
Foundation
Herrengrabenweg 56
4054 Basel, Switzerland

BERN

Hubbard Dianetics
Foundation
Muhlemattstrasse 31
Postfach 384
3000 Bern 14, Switzerland

GENEVA

Hubbard Dianetics
Foundation
12, rue des Acacias
1227 Carouge
Geneva, Switzerland

LAUSANNE

Hubbard Dianetics
Foundation
10, rue de la Madeleine
1003 Lausanne, Switzerland

ZURICH

Hubbard Dianetics
Foundation
Freilagerstrasse 11
8047 Zurich, Switzerland

AUSTRALIA

ADELAIDE

Hubbard Dianetics
  Foundation
24–28 Waymouth Street
Adelaide, South Australia
Australia 5000

BRISBANE

Hubbard Dianetics
  Foundation
106 Edward Street, 2nd Floor
Brisbane, Queensland
Australia 4000

CANBERRA

Hubbard Dianetics
  Foundation
43–45 East Row
Canberra City, ACT
Australia 2601

MELBOURNE

Hubbard Dianetics
  Foundation
42–44 Russell Street
Melbourne, Victoria
Australia 3000

PERTH

Hubbard Dianetics
  Foundation
108 Murray Street, 1st Floor
Perth, Western Australia
Australia 6000

SYDNEY

Hubbard Dianetics
  Foundation
201 Castlereagh Street
Sydney, New South Wales
Australia 2000

Advanced Organization
  Saint Hill Australia,
  New Zealand and Oceania
19–37 Greek Street
Glebe, New South Wales
Australia 2037

JAPAN

TOKYO

Hubbard Dianetics
  Foundation
2-11-7, Kita-otsuka
Toshima-ku
Tokyo, Japan 170-0004

NEW ZEALAND

AUCKLAND

Hubbard Dianetics
  Foundation
532 Ellerslie/Panmure
  Highway
Panmure, Auckland
New Zealand

AFRICA

BULAWAYO

Hubbard Dianetics
  Foundation
Southampton House,
  Suite 202
Main Street and 9th Avenue
Bulawayo, Zimbabwe

CAPE TOWN

Hubbard Dianetics
Foundation
Ground Floor, Dorlane House
39 Roeland Street
Cape Town 8001
South Africa

DURBAN

Hubbard Dianetics
Foundation
20 Buckingham Terrace
Westville, Durban 3630
South Africa

HARARE

Hubbard Dianetics
Foundation
404-409 Pockets Building
50 Jason Moyo Avenue
Harare, Zimbabwe

JOHANNESBURG

Hubbard Dianetics
Foundation
4th Floor, Budget House
130 Main Street
Johannesburg 2001
South Africa

Hubbard Dianetics
Foundation
No. 108 1st Floor,
Bordeaux Centre
Gordon Road, Corner Jan
Smuts Avenue
Blairgowrie, Randburg 2125
South Africa

PORT ELIZABETH

Hubbard Dianetics
Foundation
2 St. Christopher's
27 Westbourne Road Central
Port Elizabeth 6001
South Africa

PRETORIA

Hubbard Dianetics
Foundation
307 Ancore Building
Corner Jeppe and Esselen
Streets
Sunnyside, Pretoria 0002
South Africa

To obtain any books or lectures by L. Ron Hubbard which are not available at your local organization, contact any of the following publications organizations worldwide:

BRIDGE PUBLICATIONS, INC.
4751 Fountain Avenue
Los Angeles, California 90029
www.bridgepub.com

Rua Alfonso Celso 115
Vila Mariana São Paulo, SP
04119-000 Brazil

CONTINENTAL PUBLICATIONS LIAISON OFFICE
696 Yonge Street
Toronto, Ontario
Canada M4Y 2A7

NEW ERA PUBLICATIONS INTERNATIONAL ApS
Store Kongensgade 53
1264 Copenhagen K
Denmark
www.newerapublications.com

ERA DINÁMICA EDITORES, S.A. DE C.V.
Pablo Ucello #16
Colonia C.D. de los Deportes
Mexico, D.F.

NEW ERA PUBLICATIONS UK LTD
Saint Hill Manor
East Grinstead, West Sussex
England RH19 4JY

NEW ERA PUBLICATIONS AUSTRALIA PTY LTD
Level 1, 61–65 Wentworth
 Avenue
Surry Hills, New South Wales
Australia 2000

CONTINENTAL PUBLICATIONS PTY LTD
6th Floor, Budget House
130 Main Street
Johannesburg 2001
South Africa

NEW ERA PUBLICATIONS ITALIA S.R.L.
Via Cadorna, 61
20090 Vimodrone (MI), Italy

NEW ERA PUBLICATIONS DEUTSCHLAND GMBH
Hittfelder Kirchweg 5A
21220 Seevetal-Maschen
Germany

NEW ERA PUBLICATIONS FRANCE E.U.R.L.
14, rue des Moulins
75001 Paris, France

NUEVA ERA DINÁMICA, S.A.
C/ Montera 20, 1° dcha.
28013 Madrid, Spain

NEW ERA PUBLICATIONS JAPAN, INC.
Sakai SS bldg 2F, 4-38-15
Higashi-Ikebukuro
Toshima-ku, Tokyo, Japan
170-0013

NEW ERA PUBLICATIONS GROUP
Str. Kasatkina 16, Building 1
129301 Moscow, Russia

NEW ERA PUBLICATIONS CENTRAL EUROPEAN OFFICE
1438 Budapest
Pf. 351
Hungary

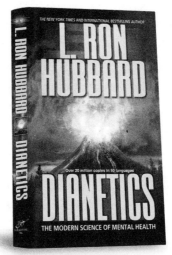